Road to Teaching

A Guide to Teacher Training, Student Teaching and Finding a Job

Eric Hougan

ISBN-13: 978-1419669071

ISBN-10: 1-4196-6907-9

Library of Congress Control Number: 2007910216

Design by Camille Yocum

Visit www.booksurge.com to order additional copies.

Acknowledgements

To begin, I must thank the most important person in my life, my wife Lesley. Her support, encouragement, and patience were instrumental in the writing of this book. Many thanks to Bríd Nowlan, my copy-editor, and Camille Yocum, my graphic designer. Your wisdom and creative ideas were greatly appreciated. Special thanks to all the people that contributed their thoughts, advice, and guidance, especially Leah Krippner, Cris Welch, Kathryn Hutchinson, and LeoNora Cohen. Last, but not least, thanks to my family, friends, teachers, colleagues, and students that have greatly influenced me throughout the years.

Contents

Excel At Student Teaching

Find Your Ideal Teacher Job

Introduction

Congratulations on beginning your career in education. Your journey to becoming a teacher will be both rewarding and challenging. Along the way, you will witness your own dramatic growth, both personally and professionally. In the end, you will be a teacher and through hard work and perseverance you will touch on and improve the lives of individuals and future generations.

My journey to becoming a teacher was a long one. When I was younger, my passion was for business. During my school years, my intense love for business never let up and I started working early on. I quickly climbed the corporate ladder. Soon after my college graduation, I traveled to India where I took a position as a project manager in a start-up company. I was quickly achieving my career and financial goals. But, a piece of me was not satisfied.

The part of my job that I found most satisfying was speaking to the groups of new hires. At every opportunity, I would drop everything and run to greet new hires before they started their training. I remember how they always looked nervous but eager to learn. During their orientation, I would calm and encourage them by sharing my experiences, and would introduce the corporate trainers. I spent more and more time in the training classrooms and finally began conducting my own classes. I loved to watch them transform into capable and successful employees. To me this was more rewarding than money or titles.

Looking back, I see this as the time when I was called to teach. After much soul searching, I decided to return to the United States to become a teacher. In doing so, I did not abandon my passion for business, but simply combined it with my new passion for teaching. My new goal was to teach business to high school students. To this day, I am still excited by the thought of making a significant difference in my students' lives through my teaching.

After some research, I applied to an established teacher education program, but this was just the beginning of my journey. My head swirled with questions about my new chosen profession. I searched for hours on the Internet to determine what certification I needed, which classes I was required to take, and how much a beginning teacher could earn. I read about the "projected shortage" of teachers. But, I could not find a single resource to guide me through the process of becoming a teacher.

The limited resources I did find usually focused on a single subject, such as building portfolios or interviewing. The vast majority of books I browsed dealt with the experiences of first year teachers. Such information and resources as were available for soon-to-be-teachers were severely fragmented. In my path to becoming a teacher, I decided that this fragmented information needed to be consolidated into an easy to read information book. It was not until I was pursuing my Masters Degree in Teaching that I began to collect information, resources, tips, and strategies to create a single resource for soon-to-be teachers.

By writing this book I hope to share pertinent information in a meaningful way with the thousands of future teachers—to provide a helpful roadmap, a big picture of sorts, for those new to the profession. This book will illustrate how to achieve the two main goals of a future teacher: to find a teaching job and become an exemplary educator.

Throughout the book, I use the term "preservice teacher," meaning any individual actively pursuing a teaching career. A preservice teacher typically goes through three phases before becoming a certified teacher: teacher education training, clinical studies (student teaching), and seeking a job. This book is organized to cover each of these important phases. It provides strategies to leverage your teacher education training, excel at student teaching, and find your ideal teaching job.

Several themes that reappear repeatedly during the process of becoming a teacher are covered throughout the book. These themes are organization, networking, and diversification. Building on these essential themes will help you make a smooth and easy transition from student to teacher

Leverage Your Teacher Education Training

Strategy 1

- - - - - - - - - - - - -

Understand the Teaching Process

**"Change is the law of life and those who look only to
the past or present are certain to miss the future."**

— John F. Kennedy

In education nothing is static; change is the one constant factor. To survive
you need to embrace this reality, as your pedagogy will be challenged regularly
by new research and ideas.

In my first year of teaching, I faced a great deal of change. I
taught over 100 new students each semester, each with diverse
learning needs. About a quarter of my students were born
outside the United States, and most of these students spoke
English as a second language. A few students had behavior or
learning disabilities, which I had no experience in dealing with. I
had to learn a little about each disability and work to meet each
student's individual education plan (IEP). The daily school schedule
changed constantly for the first three weeks—the teachers were
more confused about the schedule than the students. Lastly, the
curriculum was recently revamped and new classroom technology
was introduced.

Building a Foundation of Knowledge

How does a beginning teacher face the challenge of constant change? In short, teachers need to continually transform and reinvent themselves as professionals. This transformation is a process of acquiring knowledge about new changes and how to best address them; applying this knowledge; and, finally, evaluating how well you, as a teacher, addressed these changes.

In the first stage of your teacher education training you will be a student, building a foundation of knowledge with your class studies, research, instructional best practices, and your own experiences. In addition, you will learn about the history of education, practice various methodologies, and develop a deeper understanding of the education lexicon. Moreover, you will be:

- Observing classrooms
- Developing a curriculum to meet state standards
- Creating lesson plans that address students' special needs
- Learning about multiculturalism in the classroom
- Experimenting with instruction to meet students' multiple intelligences
- Constructing meaningful assessments

Through your studies and all of your experiences, you will begin to establish the foundation you need to build your pedagogy and teaching philosophy. By continually seeking knowledge, possessing the courage to apply best practices, and developing a habit of meaningful self-reflection, not only will you keep pace with change, but you will also become a catalyst for positive change.

Applying Your Knowledge

The next step in the teaching process is the application of knowledge: when you take what you have learned and apply it to the classroom. For a preservice teacher, student teaching is the culminating experience of years of study and work, when you transfer everything you have learned in teacher training and apply it to a real classroom.

Even before student teaching, a preservice teacher has opportunities to apply their knowledge and skills. In my teacher education program, I had practiced teaching my peers. In addition, I had practiced lesson planning and developing student assessments. I had developed the habit of listening to criticism and learning from my mistakes. Overall, I had many practice runs before student teaching, which made me more confident in my abilities as a teacher.

The application of knowledge is a critical piece in the teaching process. You must be open to new ideas, paradigms, and pedagogical best practices, and be willing to challenge yourself to apply those in your classroom. In the application stage, you begin to define yourself as a teacher that takes risks and puts forth his or her best effort.

Reflection on Continual Improvement

As a preservice teacher, constantly improving, you will be doing a great deal of reflection. A reflective teacher stays current with changes in his or her field, continuously looks to the future, and is driven to excel. Reflection gives you the opportunity to evaluate the effectiveness of your pedagogy during the application stage. In other words, you will examine what worked and what didn't work when you tried to apply something, such as an instructional strategy or a new discipline technique. You will also consider how you can improve your teaching practice to produce even greater results in the form of student learning and motivation in the future.

Example

You have devised a new way of incorporating digital cameras into a lesson, based on a case study you read. You think this lesson will be of high interest and meet some of the learning styles of your students. You are excited about the lesson, you felt it was successful—now what do you do?

First, you need to define what success is, in the context of your lesson. Does success mean that the students were engaged? Does it mean they have learned all, most, or some of your lesson objectives? Once you have defined success, write down the highlights of the lesson, such as:

- High student involvement

- State standards were met

- Low discipline problems

- Demonstration that students met learning objectives

- High interest in the subject among the students

- Learned about new technology

Next, consider how the lesson could be improved? For example, you could provide written objectives and instructions for the lesson to the students at the beginning of the lesson. Alternatively, you could create a follow-up activity that readdresses the lesson's objectives.

This reflection stage should not be burdensome. Sometimes just jotting down quick notes on what you could improve is sufficient. The main point is to find a system that allows you to adjust and improve your lessons. Practical strategies on becoming a more reflective teacher are provided later in the book (see Strategy 26).

By learning from your experiences, you will continue to build your knowledge foundation and the teaching process will continue. This process is conceptualized in the following diagram:

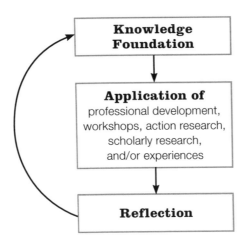

Strategy 2

Save and Organize Information With Purpose

"The trouble with organizing a thing is that pretty soon folks get to paying more attention to the organization than to what they're organized for."

— Laura Ingalls Wilder

During your teaching training, you will receive a large amount of information from an assortment of resources – instructors, peers, and your own experiences – on everything from special education to bilingual education to school reform. At times, you will feel overwhelmed by it all. You can help yourself by organizing this information with purpose, effectively building your knowledge foundation, and allowing you to easily access and reference this information in the future when you want to apply it. An ineffective organizational process will just leave you with piles of meaningless papers strategically stored under the bed or in the closet.

An important skill we educators can instill into our students is the ability to capture information and gather personal meaning from it. Before we can teach this skill, we must first master it. This book is designed to help the preservice (future) teacher to become organized, so you can recall information quickly, and, more importantly, be able to extract meaningful knowledge from it.

> In just one class in my teacher education program, I was handed over 60 articles on 20 different topics. There were 20 students in my class, and we each had to prepare a presentation on one of those 20 topics, and provide the rest of the class at least three

other research articles. I almost collapsed under the information overload. What was I going to do? Many of my peers simply used the trashcan to meet their organizational needs—disposing of anything that seemed superfluous. But, the information my peers presented was useful, and I knew that at some point in my teaching career I might need it. The problem was I did not have an effective organizational strategy. I was all over the place, like the information I was gathering. I had a few articles in one class folder, some saved in another class folder, and even more stored in my flash drive.

An effective organization strategy can save you a lot of future frustration. First, develop a filing system. Your filing system should work for you. Remember to organize with purpose. If you are more likely to recall an article by its topic, you might want to group your articles, research, observations, etc by the topic rather than in class folders.

An electronic system will allow you to save all you information in one location for an indefinite amount of time. Complete all your work on your computer, and try to get all your information (research papers, etc.) electronically, via email or compact disc.

A physical system of file folders should mirror your electronic system, so you can easily access information in either place.

Here are a few organizational strategies for your computer and/or physical folders:

- Create class folders. Once you complete work for a particular class, save the material in its corresponding folder.

- Manage information based on themes. Perhaps you have written about student journaling in several classes. Instead of saving each piece of work in each separate class folder, it might be easier to save all works regarding journaling in one folder named "Journaling."

- Create folders based on your teacher education activities. For instance, you might want to save all your classroom observation notes in one folder, regardless of which class you completed them for.

Now that you have your computer set-up for electronic information and a filing cabinet ready for physical papers, there is still the problem of having too little time to sift through so many papers. Imagine you are in your first year of teaching. You have a student that has a learning disability and you want to read up on that disability and determine if there are approaches you can take to meet the student's needs. Remembering that you have some research and information from your teacher-training program, you go to your file cabinet to find a file labeled "Exceptional Students." There are over a dozen articles and research packets in the folder. You do not have the time to read or even review each article in search of that specific learning disability your student may have.

An extremely effective way of tackling this problem is adding notes to each article or research packet. As you review an article in class, take a few minutes to jot down some notes on the article's thesis and any meaningful points that might be of use in the future. You can write your notes on the article's cover page, or on a sticky note. Here are some suggestions to help you write concise, useful notes:

- In 1-2 sentences write "The purpose of this article is …"

- Using bullet points write, "This article is meaningful because …"

Develop this organizational strategy into a habit, but not a chore. You do not want to kill yourself by making extensive notes on each article you receive. Rather, write something that will help to jog your memory, so when you search your files in the future you will quickly recall whether this article will assist in your inquiry. This strategy will assist you throughout your career because you are:

1) Forcing yourself to synthesize the information when the information is fresh

2) Continuing to build a meaningful knowledge foundation for future applications

Strategy 3

- - - - - - - - - - -

Capture Those Fleeting Thoughts

"By three methods we may learn wisdom:
first, by reflection, which is noblest;
second, by imitation, which is easiest; and
third, by experience, which is the most bitter."

— Confucius

Effective organization goes beyond putting papers into labeled folders to synthesizing information, capturing your thoughts and feelings, and deriving personal meaning from that information.

Like our students, we learn best by practicing, observing, and reflecting than through lectures and handouts. For instance, you are likely to learn more sitting in the corner of a classroom observing a master teacher for an hour than you might learn in four hours of lecture in your methodology class. In this classroom observation, you may note the colorful walls decked with students' achievements. You observe how the teacher applies discipline in a dignified and fair manner, careful never to humiliate or attack the students; notice how she uses proximity when teaching, and gives appropriate wait time to hear a student's answer; and hear her praise the students' comments and work. You observe the challenging lesson with its clear objective and assessment. You feel the respectful relationship between students and teacher. This experience is meaningful and relevant. You begin to reflect on how you would apply these strategies in your own classroom.

Writing a journal is one of the most effective ways to capture your feelings, observations, and thoughts in an organized manner, so that you can put them to good use in the future. Master teachers report that their journals are critical components of their professional development. They find that a journal is a helpful tool for evaluating and improving their work, and recording their professional growth over time. It can also help with stress management.

I found writing in a journal particularly useful in organizing all my classroom observations. As part of my teacher training, I had to complete 100 hours of clinical observations in different schools, different classrooms (mainstream, inclusive, etc.), and with different teachers. While doing so I worked hard to identify at least one best practice in each class that I could use in my own teaching. At the end of each observation, I recorded my impressions of the class in my journal. To organize my thoughts, I developed a list of questions:

- What type of classroom did I observe, i.e. mainstream, resource, inclusive?

- How is the classroom arranged and/or organized?

- What strategies does the teacher use to address the student's specific needs?

- Are the lessons collaboratively planned across disciplines?

- For special education, what support services were utilized?

- Any personal impressions, such as …?

Sample Journal Entry

The first impression that I have from my observations was in a mainstream classroom with a general education teacher and a special education teacher. My overriding impression is the special education teacher was not fully utilized. I was dismayed by the fact that the special education teacher and the general education teachers did not collaborate in their planning, despite that they knew it was a best practice and, ultimately, would benefit all the students. For instance, I noted that one student with ADD finished his work in nearly half the time than his classmate did. I cannot comment how accurate his work was, but I do know that he began to act out once he became bored with having nothing to do. In using collaborative planning, the general education teacher and the special education teacher could have developed new and challenging class work for when this student finished normal class work earlier than the rest of the class. This would improve the student's performance and behavior.

The biggest challenge we all face with keeping a journal is carving out time to write every day. As it is such a critical tool in professional development, you should strive to make writing in your journal a habit. Here are a few suggestions to help you:

1) Keep a spiral notebook and pen next to your bed. Before you go to sleep, unwind by unloading all your thoughts into your journal for about 10-15 minutes.

2) Schedule daily writing time, for example, set aside 10-15 minutes during your planning periods.

3) Make notes directly after a class you have taken or taught.

4) Create or join a web log (blog) and post entries regularly. Then, read the advice and words of encouragement posted from other teachers reading your blog. To start a free blog, go to www.blogger.com.

If you encounter writer's block because of a grueling day with students then use writing prompts. Here are several thought-provoking, writing prompts (Thompson, 2002):

- Advice you have received
- A brief summary of your day
- Funny things you hear or see

- New ideas

- Mistakes you will not repeat

- Your goals

- Impressions about other teachers and students

- Procedures you need to change

If you include journal writing as part of your daily routine, you will continue to be active in the teaching process by building on your knowledge foundation. In a short time, you will start to see significant personal and professional growth. Ultimately, this will help you to create a better learning environment for your students.

Strategy 4

_ _ _ _ _ _ _ _ _ _ _

Organize Your Reading

"I took a speed reading course and read 'War and Peace' in twenty minutes. It involves Russia."

— Woody Allen

Teachers are expected to stay abreast of current research. Doing so means reading books and scholarly papers. Organize your reading as you go by writing a list of all the relevant books and articles you have read on education. The list of reading should include:

- Title of the book/paper

- Author(s) name

- Subject matter

- Application to teaching (e.g. methodology, classroom management, etc.)

Under each entry, write a short synopsis of the work and how it might apply to your teaching. Save your reading list electronically, on your computer, or create a folder for it in your filing cabinet, or do both.

Maintaining a reading list has several advantages. You may be asked in an interview to discuss some education related literature you have recently read. This interview question is especially common for reading intensive teaching positions, such as Language Arts. Before your interview, you can refresh your memory by briefly reviewing your reading list. You can also include your reading list as part of your portfolio to demonstrate a motivation for professional excellence.

Your reading list is also your personal reference library. Suppose that after three years of teaching you have to teach a class that includes a student with autism. You remember reading a book that could shed a great deal of insight into the world of autism. By simply referring to your reading list, you will quickly discover the author and title of the book.

Strategy 5

Become an Expert on a Particular Concept

"What's the use of running if you are not on the right road."

— German proverb

In one of my graduate classes, the professor relayed to us some advice that she had received when she was in college, and that she considered one of the most important pieces of advice she had received in her career: organize your studies, whenever possible, around a central theme. Whenever you are given an opportunity to choose a research topic, stick to one education topic of interest to you, such as interdisciplinary teams, cooperative learning, multiple intelligences, or special education. By building on a central theme throughout your academic career, you:

- Become an expert on that topic, building on your knowledge with each class you take and teach

- Reduce your workload, by using your research for more than one project

- Build references and research that may be used later for a graduate degree

This concept of sticking to one theme, at which you become expert, resonated with me because of my business background. In his best-selling business book Good to Great, Jim Collins (2001) identifies this as a common element among many high-performing organizations. Collins recommends developing your theme or area of concentration from your answers to these three questions:

- What are you deeply passionate about?

- What can you be the best at?

- What drives your research, studies, and/or pedagogy?

I thought about my professor's advice and the research presented in <u>Good to Great</u> and decided my central theme would be interdisciplinary teaming—for two reasons. The school where I intended to student teach practiced interdisciplinary teaming, and I had extensive experience working in teams in the business world. I used interdisciplinary teaming as the driver for my research and studies. By completing some teacher education courses, I began to build a wealth of resources on the topic, each class adding a new perspectives to the topic, as outlined in Table 5.1 below.

Table 5.1

Courses Taken	Added Perspective
Adolescent Development	Researched how interdisciplinary teams contributed to a sense of community and helped meet the adolescent's need for belonging.
Exceptional Children	Researched the benefits of interdisciplinary teams in special education.
Quantitative Research	Added quantitative research and a literature review of the benefits of interdisciplinary teams.
Qualitative Research	Added qualitative research and a literature review of the benefits of interdisciplinary teams.

Once you find a topic that interests you and you begin to research it, remember to organize it in a manner that makes the most sense to you. It might be best to create a single folder to keep all your work and research together (see Strategy 2).

Strategy 6

Jumpstart Your Teacher Portfolio

"The life which is not examined is not worth living."

— Plato

A working portfolio is a set of documents that reflects your professional growth. You should begin to develop it during your teacher education program and your student teaching, then edit and refine it as you grow. A portfolio is useful when applying for a job, obtaining a higher certification or degree, and examining and reflecting on your own pedagogy.

Before you can present your portfolio to a hiring principal, or send it in for certification, it must be organized and made presentable. Remember your portfolio is a reflection of who you are. If your portfolio is chaotic then those reviewing your portfolio will more than likely assume that you are too.

If you have created an efficient organization system (see Strategy 2) and reflected on your personal growth (see Strategy 3), you are half way to a complete portfolio. A working portfolio of a preservice teacher might include the following sections:

- Cover Letter

- Belief and Philosophy Statement (see Strategy 18)

- Observation Reflections

- Resume (see Strategy 38)

- Professional Reflections (see Strategy 3)

- Annotated Reading List (see Strategy 4)

It is essential to begin building your portfolio at an early stage. Collect all these materials in a new 3-ring binder. They can be added to and changed as you progress through your teacher training. Later, when you begin your student teaching, you will need to collect your students' work and sample lesson plans, both good and bad.

Electronic Portfolio

I am often asked about electronic portfolios. School principals have told me that while an electronic portfolio is a good idea in theory, in reality they have very little time to spend logging into a website, entering electronic pass codes, and then clicking the various hyperlinks associated with your portfolio. Yet, creating and maintaining a professional electronic portfolio is essential in case a principal is interested in perusing your work.

Why have an electronic portfolio rather than a paper portfolio? Electronic portfolios have two benefits. First, they are extremely easy to compile and organize, as you can scan in any relevant or important documents, such as class observations. Second, they show principals that you are comfortable with computer technology. In addition, an electronic portfolio is easily accessible. It can be viewed by anyone, anywhere in the world, with a computer and an Internet connection.

Privacy

Since your portfolio will include student work or student pictures be sure to protect their privacy and secure the permission of the student's legal guardian to use such work or photographs. Or, you can black out or erase any personal information on the student work, such as the student's name, and include only pictures in which the students' faces cannot be distinguished.

If you are using an electronic portfolio, protect your own privacy by carefully reviewing the provider's privacy agreement to determine how your information will be shared. At the very least, a password should be needed for others to gain access to your portfolio.

Strategy 7

- - - - - - - - - - - - -

Confront the Reality of the Job Market

"When you start with an honest and diligent effort to determine the truth of your situation, the right decisions often become self-evident."

— Jim Collins, Good to Great

As a preservice teacher, you need to understand the current job market and how to best position yourself to find your dream job. To do so, you must look past the simple statistics, headlines, and news reports.

Long-term trends point to a teacher shortage. A publication from the State Higher Education Executive Officer's Project describes a projected need of 2.2 million new teachers over the next 10 years (Hirsch, 2001). The 1999-2000 NCES Schools and Staffing Survey explains some of the factors that led to such dramatic predictions:

- Between 2000 and 2008, enrollment in public high schools is expected to increase by 4%

- More than 25% of teachers are at least 50 years old and the median age is 44

- Many school reform efforts call for class-size reduction, which requires more teachers

On the surface, these statistics look very promising for a future teacher, and you might think that every school district across the nation is scrambling to find teachers. However, teacher shortages are mostly occurring in a few regions and disciplines:

- States with high growth, such as California, Nevada, Texas, Florida, and North Carolina

- Predominately in urban areas

- High-need content areas, such math, science, bilingual programs, and special education

If you fit into one of these categories you may have a better chance of landing a teaching job, but the brutal reality is everyone still faces competition. Principals still receive multiple applications, even for high-need teaching positions. Robert Pollock (2001), a principal who has interviewed hundreds of teachers, advises, "Do not confuse a teacher shortage to mean an absence of competition. Granted, there is more competition in some districts than others, yet there is always competition. You need strategies that will place you in front of that competition." This book will provide you with strategies you can use during preservice teaching to differentiate yourself from your peers, through your interests, education, and experiences, so that you will be well placed to find your dream job.

Strategy 8

Explore Other Interests

Develop a passion for learning.
If you do, you will never cease to grow.

— Anthony J. D'Angelo

I entered the university to become a high school teacher. I believed that high school students would be more mature and I would be able to facilitate higher level of thinking in those classes. As I completed my classes and observation hours in middle schools, I began to appreciate the middle school students. Yes, the student maturity level at middle schools is slightly less than at high school. But, I enjoyed the wackiness and goofiness that can go along with being a middle-school teacher. Moreover, I loved working in teams, creating a sense of community among the students and teachers, and having greater freedom of creativity with my pedagogy. I changed my initial student teaching assignment from a high school U.S. history class to a middle school social studies class. My original thought that I only wanted to teach at the high school level was shattered after exploring other teaching opportunities.

Through your teacher education training, you will be exposed to a wide variety of topics and experiences. You may find over time that your teaching preference and goals change. Since teaching requires energy and dedication, you should choose to teach something you love and are passionate about. Otherwise, you will not last in the profession. Keep an open mind and allow yourself to explore new areas of education and you might find yourself on a different path to teaching.

Strategy 9

- - - - - - - - - - - -

Differentiate Yourself Through Education

**The beautiful thing about learning is
that no one can take it away from you.**

— B.B. King

Principals are looking for teachers that are flexible, dedicated, and an asset to the school in more than one way. In a competitive job market, you must seek ways to stand out from your peers—one great way is through education.

Imagine you are the hiring principal. You have an open high school Social Studies position and you have narrowed the field to two highly qualified candidates:

Candidate A is a recent graduate who interviewed well and had a great portfolio that illustrated her pedagogy and professional growth. She is certified to teach Social Studies.

Candidate B is also a recent graduate. She interviewed well and had a fantastic portfolio full of lesson plans and student work. She is certified to teach Social Studies and English language learners (ELL).

Examining both of these highly qualified candidates, which one would you choose? The principal would hire Candidate B. Candidate B is a greater asset to the school because she can teach Social Studies and, if necessary, teach ELL Social Studies. She would be a fantastic resource, especially if the school's student demographics are trending toward ELL students.

Evaluate your own situation. Which candidate would you typify, A or B? Take a moment and answer these questions:

- Are you specializing in special education and/or ELL?

- Are you a male seeking an elementary teaching position?

- Are you going into a discipline that is in high demand, e.g., sciences and math?

- Have you done anything to set yourself apart from other job seekers?

If you cannot answer "yes" to at least one of these questions, I recommend taking additional courses to improve your chances of being hired in the school of your choice. Moreover, strive to become certified in more than one teaching area. Not only will you broaden your educational credentials, you will become a better teacher.

> I learned a great deal from the additional ELL courses I took. Now that I teach in a school where 10–20% of the students are English language learners, my training allows me to do a better job at meeting their social and learning needs.

Additional certification also provides you with more opportunities. After some years of teaching, you may decide you need a change. That additional certification will allow you to pursue new teaching opportunities, perhaps even within the same school.

The additional coursework may also increase your income by pushing you up in the pay schedule once you begin teaching. Of course, this will differ from state to state and district to district.

Strategy 10

- - - - - - - - - - - -

Discover the Benefits of High Need Areas

**A tax loophole is something that benefits the other guy.
If it benefits you, it is tax reform.**

— Russell B. Long

There is a high demand for teachers in some states and school districts, for a number of reasons, including, an increase in student population, a change in student demographics, high teacher turnover, large numbers of teachers that are not qualified to teach, and new legislative requirements. This may be to your advantage. Explore the pay and benefits of your local school districts and, if you are willing to move, other states. Benefits offered in high demand areas range from $5,000 sign-on bonuses to housing assistance programs, and may come from various sources, including local, state, or federal governments, and school districts

Loan Forgiveness

One little known teacher benefit is the Federal Government's Teacher Loan Forgiveness Program. This program grants loan forgiveness of up to $17,500 for teachers in certain specialties, and up to $5,000 for other teachers who teach for five years in low-income schools. Table 10.1 provides an overview of the program.

Table 10.1

How does the Teacher Loan Forgiveness Program work?

If you have five consecutive years of qualifying teaching service in a designated "low-income" school by the U.S. Department of Education and your service began on or after *October 30, 2004*:

You may receive up to $5,000 in loan forgiveness if, as certified by the Chief Administrative Officer of the school where you were employed, you were:

- A full-time elementary school teacher who demonstrated knowledge and teaching skills in reading, writing, mathematics, and other areas of the elementary school curriculum

- A **full-time secondary school teacher** who taught in a subject area that was relevant to your academic major

You may receive up to $17,500 in loan forgiveness if, as certified by the Chief Administrative Officer of the school where you were employed, you were:

- A highly qualified full-time **mathematics** or **science teacher** in an eligible secondary school

- A highly qualified **special education** teacher whose primary responsibility was to provide special education to children with disabilities, and you were teaching children with disabilities that corresponded to your area of special education training and have demonstrated knowledge and teaching skills in the content areas of the curriculum that you were teaching

To learn more details of this loan forgiveness program visit:

www.studentaid.ed.gov (you may have to search using "teacher loan forgiveness") or call 1-800-433-3243

Housing Assistance

Another benefit to teachers is the Good Neighbor program of the U.S. Department of Housing and Urban Development (HUD). It encourages teachers to purchase houses in low to moderate-income neighborhoods. Under this program, homebuyers receive a 50% discount on the list price, so you could purchase a $250,000 home for $125,000. See Table 10.2 below for more information on this program.

Table 10.2

What are general requirements of the Good Neighbor program?

The program is open to any person "employed full-time by a public school, private school, or federal, state, county, or municipal educational agency as a state-certified classroom teacher or administrator in grades K-12." Participants must certify that they are employed by an educational agency that serves the school district/jurisdiction in which the home they are purchasing is located. Moreover, you cannot own another home when you close on your Good Neighbor home. Lastly, you must agree to live in the home for 3 years.

How do I participate in the Good Neighbor program?

Qualifying property is listed and sold exclusively over the Internet. Properties are single-family homes located in Revitalization Areas.
Properties available through the program are marked with a special Good Neighbor button.

HUD requires that you sign a **second mortgage** and note for the discount amount. No interest or payments are required on this "silent second" provided you fulfill the **three-year occupancy requirement**.

To learn more details of home assistance program visit:

www.hud.gov/offices/hsg/sfh/reo/goodn/tnd.cfm

Other Benefits

Many states have adopted additional incentives to recruit and retain qualified teachers. Call your state's education office or visit their website to determine what incentives are offered.

Strategy 11

Go Beyond "Highly Qualified"

**To be idle is a short road to death and to be diligent is a way of life;
foolish people are idle, wise people are diligent.**

— Buddha

As a preservice teacher, you may hear a lot of talk about the No Child Left
Behind (NCLB) Act. This federal law requires that all teachers in core academic
areas must be "highly qualified" by the end of the 2005–2006 school year. The
basic requirements for a highly qualified teacher are:

- Hold a bachelor's degree

- Obtain full state certification, which can be "alternative certification"

- Demonstrate subject-matter competency in the core academic
  subjects taught

What exactly is the No Child Left Behind Act?

According to the U.S. Department of Education, the NCLB Act of 2001...

> "...Incorporates the principles and strategies proposed by President
> Bush. These include increased accountability for States, school
> districts, and schools; greater choice for parents and students,
> particularly those attending low-performing schools; more flexibility
> for States and local educational agencies (LEA's) in the use of Federal
> education dollars; and a stronger emphasis on reading, especially for
> our youngest children."

You can differentiate yourself from other recent graduates by moving beyond the traditional definition of a highly qualified teacher, as described in the NCLB Act. I believe the NCLB's definition of a "highly qualified teacher" is lacking one important component: that the teacher demonstrate strength in pedagogy. A highly qualified teacher is one that demonstrates both competency in subject matter and effective pedagogy. Many preservice teachers who follow the traditional teacher education programs and complete their certification are strong in pedagogy, but weak in subject matter. Whereas someone entering into the teaching profession from industry or the field of study they want to teach may be strong in the subject matter, but weak in pedagogy.

Use your preservice teaching experience to identify and strengthen your weak areas and to grow professionally beyond the traditional definition of "highly qualified." After school or during the summer take advantage of any and all opportunities to gain further insight into your content area or to strengthen your pedagogy. Your efforts will pay off by creating meaningful work experiences that will differentiate you from other job seekers.

I did not consciously think that by taking jobs substituting or working in summer student programs I would increase my chances of being hired. Really, I did it because I love teaching and I wanted to become better at it. Yet as I began to prepare my resume and practice for interviews, I realized how valuable all these experiences were. While substitute teaching for bouncing third graders and vivacious middle school students, I had the opportunity to experiment with some of the best-practice pedagogy I learned in my program studies. These experiences also shaped me as a teacher and gave me time to develop my own approach and style.

During the summers, I happily participated as an instructor in the federally funded program called Upward Bound that supports students preparing for college. Teaching in this program gave me a chance to become more competent at teaching in my content area of business.

All these experiences, in one-way or another, helped shape me into a highly qualified teacher.

In summary, avoid the temptation to be idle during those off days or during the summer. Instead, look for opportunities to excel and grow.

Examples

To Become More Competent in your Subject Matter

- Volunteer in an organization that researches or supports your content area. For example, if you are an art teacher you could volunteer at the local art gallery or museum. You could then meet local artists that may later be helpful in your own classroom.

- Find an internship or a job in your content area.

- Teach a workshop or a course at the local community college.

To Develop a Stronger Pedagogy

- Substitute teach in your local schools. This is really the best way to learn about teaching and the different schools in your community.

- Volunteer or work in student summer programs. Such programs as TRIO Upward Bound can be found in hundreds of communities across the United States.

- Tutor and mentor students. You can work with local private tutoring companies or advertise your own services.

Strategy 12

- - - - - - - - - -

Learn From Your Work Experience

**In wisdom gathered over time I have found that
every experience is a form of exploration.**

— Ansel Adams

Work experience looks fantastic on a resume and helps you answer such
interview questions as:

- What were some important lessons you learned from your experiences?

- What are the skills you possess that will assist you as a teacher? Why?

- What is a challenge you faced and how you did you overcome it?

- How are you different from the other job candidates?

Your work experiences provide an additional and unique window for interviewers
to evaluate you. Use this to your advantage. Differentiate yourself from other
candidates by talking about your work experiences and demonstrating how
those experiences make you a stronger teacher. Think back to your work
experiences and connect your experience to teaching. For instance, in your job,
were you a team player or leader? This is important because as an educator you
will be collaborating with colleagues or may have to lead a new initiative at the
school. In your work experience, did you prove yourself an innovator? Explain
to the interviewer how you will utilize those experiences and skills to maximize
student learning. Lastly, was your line of work in the field you plan to teach?
Having first hand, real-life experience in your content area makes you a stronger
teacher by bringing unique insights another teacher may not have.

Extracting meaning from your work experience and reflecting on how it applies to your teaching is a meaningful activity in preparing for an interview. Think back on your experiences, answer the questions above in your journal, and determine how your experiences will better position you as a job candidate.

Strategy 13

Benefit From Networking

**I didn't really want to be an actress but
I had some connections so when I got tired of waitressing,
I started doing commercials for Twix and Burger King.**

— Lea Thompson

By the end of your teacher education program, you will have relevant and meaningful information readily available, and you will have focused your studies around a central theme. Furthermore, you will have begun to set yourself apart from other job seekers by diversifying your educational and work backgrounds. Now, let us explore the third essential theme of this book—networking. Networking plays an important role in obtaining a teaching job. Substitute teaching provides one of the best opportunities for networking in the education field.

What is networking?

In The Networking Survival Guide: Get the Success You Want by Tapping into the People You Know, Diane Darling (2003) defines networking as:

"… being active: That's the ing part of the word. It requires your participation. Our network is the group of people who want us to be safe and secure—personally and professionally. It is those who are willing to lend a hand, share an idea, champion our efforts, and when appropriate, challenge us to new heights."

Darling further explains that networking includes:

- Getting the help you need, when you need it, from those from whom you need it
- Sharing of knowledge and contacts
- Getting more done with less effort
- Building relationships before you need them
- Helping others

When I first began to build my work experience, I quickly realized the value of networking. I began my work experience by substitute teaching in two large local school districts. For the first month, I was called to substitute teach only twice. I could not understand why I was not called more often. It was extremely frustrating because not only could I not get my foot in the door, but also I was not making enough to pay my bills. When I had gone through the process of becoming certified as a substitute teacher, I was told that there was a great need for subs. If there was a great need and low supply of subs, then why wasn't I being called more often?

The reason is that teachers would request certain substitutes or prearrange the substitute teacher assignments. It was not first come first serve. Rather a select number of substitute teachers were being called day after day to teach. It was not the fault of those substitute teachers, but rather they were being chosen because they had proven their ability to perform in their job. The regular teachers trusted them and saw them as a safe choice.

As frustrated as I was, I knew it would take time before I could prove myself and build up a network of teacher contacts.

Here are helpful tips to build a teacher network during substitute teaching:

- In the school, get to meet other teachers by greeting them or asking a simple question. Inevitably, the conversation will turn to asking you who you are substituting for.

- When you substitute, provide superb, detailed class notes for the teacher, including accurate attendance records, and names of students that were helpful and those that were disrespectful. Don't think that by talking about something that went wrong in the classroom the regular teacher will think of you as incompetent and will not call you back. On the contrary, teachers want to know exactly happened while they were away to make sure the students are behaving to their expectations.

- Leave your contact information (name, phone number, email, and/or your substitute teacher ID # if you have one), so they can request you again.

- Mingle in the teacher's lounge and hallway. Remember, you are creating a network of teachers. These are the people who may call on you later, to substitute in their classroom, or may provide you with some details of a possible job opening. See everyone as part of your network.

Over the course of a few months, I was repeatedly requested by teachers I previously substitute taught for and by teachers that I met at lunch. I was happy, and so was my budget.

Networking is about being active and participating. Understandably, networking does not come naturally to everyone. At times joining a conversation can be tricky and small talk can seem trivial. Networking can be difficult, but this is not an excuse not to try. If you are frustrated with being outside the network of local teachers, channel your energy to breaking in and building your own network. There are some simple ways to start. Sit at the lunch table with other teachers. Join in on conversations. Introduce yourself to an unfamiliar face. Eventually, with some patience and tenacity, you will start to see the fruits of your labor and you will become more confident in dealing with people.

Strategy 14

Create Face-time With Administrators

Facing it, always facing it, that's the way to get through. Face it.

— Joseph Conrad

While you are substitute teaching, visiting a school, or observing classrooms make it a point to have face-time with administrators, without becoming a nuisance. Meet them in a casual setting, such as the school lunchroom. You should become a familiar face in the school building. Greet teachers and administrators in the hallways as they hustle and bustle back and forth between classes. Volunteer to make visits to the office to pick up such things as mail or supplies. While most of the administrators probably will not remember you by name, in an interview, they will recall your friendly face as having some context to the school, and this gives you an advantage over other, less well-known, job applicants.

Strategy 15

- - - - - - - - - - -

Manage Your Contacts

If you can organize your kitchen, you can organize your life.

— Louis Parrish

One valuable skill I transferred from my business experience to teaching was keeping accurate records of my contacts. As you begin to network and meet more and more people, it is a superb idea to begin assembling some type of organizational system for your contact information.

There are many ways to do this. For instance, I know people (my mother included) that like to write names and contact information on index cards and keep them in a shoebox. While this may work well for some, there are also many more up-to-date organization strategies. If you have already created a well-organized file system on your personal computer, I would recommend storing all your contacts in a spreadsheet, like Microsoft Excel. This allows you to backup your contact list and use special functions like sorting. Below is an example of how I assembled my contacts using Excel.

Table 15.1

Sample Contact Using a Spreadsheet						
Column A	B	C	D	E	F	G
Name	Title	Organization	Address	Phone	Email	Notes
John Doe	Principal	Seattle High	123 Seattle High Ave.	206-555-5403	john.doe@ seattle.edu	Met 5/5/06. Told me of a possible job opening in Fall. Follow-up in July.

A web-based application may be an alternative platform to construct your contact list. You can create contact lists in free-email accounts like Yahoo, Hotmail, and Gmail. Plaxo is another great organizational tool (www.plaxo.com). With Plaxo, you can input information from anywhere you have Internet access, so you do not have to be at your personal computer. Plaxo also synchronizes with your other contact lists (Hotmail, Yahoo, Outlook, etc.), so it can serve as a universal contact list. Through Plaxo, you can easily provide your undated contact information to others and retrieve current contact information from them.

Once you have established and recorded your contact, stay in touch with your network with regular updates. Simply send an email every so often (3 months) to say hello, tell them about changes in your life, and ask about them. This will allow you to keep in contact and build a relationship before you need them.

Strategy 16

- - - - - - - - - - - -

Consider Everyone Part of Your Network

Call it a clan, call it a network, call it a tribe, call it a family.
Whatever you call it, whoever you are, you need one.

— Jane Howard

Think for a moment about your family, neighbors, friends, and former colleagues. Now ask yourself: do any of these people have ties or connections to education? For instance, your neighbor may be the principal of your local high school, or your best friend's mother may be a teacher. Expand your thinking to include those outside your circle of friends and colleagues. Include people from all areas of your life, from church to clubs you may belong to. Make a list of anyone that comes to mind and note how he or she is connected to education. This is a critical building block in establishing your network.

By listing people that you may have strong or weak connections to, you are increasing the likelihood of getting the teaching job you want. The importance of a social network in finding a job is illustrated by the classic 1974 study Getting a Job by the sociologist Mark Gravovetter (Gladwell, 2000). By examining the employment history of several hundred professionals, Gravovetter concluded that 56% found a job through a personal connection. Only 20% of the study subjects found their jobs by applying directly to prospective employers. For those that found their jobs through personal connections, the majority of these connections were "weak ties." Fifty six percent saw their contacts only "occasionally," while 28% saw their contact "rarely."

From this study, it appears more likely that you will find a job from someone that you occasionally see, than by applying directly to a school. Consider anyone a possible contact, and by building these contacts, you, a future job candidate, will improve your chances of finding your dream job.

Strategy 17

- - - - - - - - - - - -

Network Within Your Teacher Education Program

A teacher affects eternity; he can never tell where his influence stops.

— Henry Adams

Your colleagues in your teacher education program provide another rich opportunity for networking. Together, your peers and professors encompass diverse experiences and backgrounds that could be of great benefit to you.

> In my teacher education program, I developed many friendships with other preservice teachers. I know they would assist me if I needed help, and they know I would do the same for them. My network of friends alone represents 13 high schools in seven different districts. This was helpful when I was looking for work, as my friends would send me emails to let me know about upcoming job openings in their schools or districts. Not only would my friends put in a good word with the administration, but such advance notification also allowed me to be one of first to apply for that teaching position.

Your professors can also be a valuable part of your network. Many of my professors were former teachers or administrators and were willing to share pertinent information. Your college faculty can provide insights into the job market, such as which schools/districts are hiring, and can also tell you what principals look for in job candidates. This information can give a critical edge to a preservice teacher.

In one of my courses, I really connected with one of my professors that I greatly respected. The professor answered my questions, addressed my concerns, and validated many of the feelings a preservice teacher has. Additionally, the professor provided excellent feedback on how to improve my cover letter and resume, and even provided me with an outstanding recommendation letter.

Excel at Student Teaching

Strategy 18

Develop Your Philosophy and Core Values

**The philosophy of the schoolroom in one generation
will be the philosophy of government in the next.**

— Abraham Lincoln

Congratulations! You have made to the next stage in your preservice training: student teaching. Now you will take everything you have learned from your teacher education training and apply it to a real classroom. In anticipation of student teaching, countless questions are probably rolling around in your mind.

All your questions are valid, but you can go crazy trying to think of all the possible answers and outcomes. In this section of the book, you will learn strategies that will prepare you for student teaching. It all begins with developing a sound personal philosophy of education. The above quote from Abraham Lincoln illustrates the importance of your education philosophy, as it affects future generations and shapes society.

What is an Education Philosophy Statement?

An education philosophy statement is the bedrock of any master teacher; it encapsulates the principles and beliefs you bring to your teaching and creates the foundation and framework from which your classroom decisions are made. Once established, your philosophy will for the most part remain the same, but it will change some over time to reflect your teaching experience and ongoing professional development. Since it is your bedrock, it is important to understand your education philosophy before you begin your journey in teaching.

Write an Education Philosophy Statement

Writing a philosophy takes a lot of time and reflection. To begin, reflect on the following questions and write your responses in your journal:

- What motivated you to go into teaching?
- What values and beliefs would an ideal teacher have?
- What are your beliefs about students, learning, behavior, respect, schools, general education, etc.?
- What changes would you like to see in our education system?
- What values do you want to model for the students inside and outside the classroom?
- Of your beliefs, which ones are non-negotiable?

When you begin writing your education philosophy statement remember that it is about YOU and YOUR BELIEFS. Avoid writing educational buzzwords and phrases to just make it sound better. The best way to start is with "I believe..." Keep it short—no longer than one page of single-spaced type.

Here are two sample education philosophy statements from preservice teachers at the Ohio State University College of Education (Cohen & Gelbrich, 1999). See how the formatting and approach expresses each writer's individuality. Although very different, both are effective and well written. But, it takes time to write a concise, effective statement of philosophy, so do not give up on your first try.

Table 18.2

Sample 1

I believe that each child is a unique individual who needs a secure, caring, and stimulating atmosphere in which to grow and mature emotionally, intellectually, physically, and socially. It is my desire as an educator to help students meet their fullest potential in these areas by providing an environment that is safe, supports risk-taking, and invites a sharing of ideas. There are three elements that I believe are conducive to establishing such an environment, (1) the teacher acting as a guide, (2) allowing the child's natural curiosity to direct his/her learning, and (3) promoting respect for all things and all people.

When the teacher's role is to guide, providing access to information rather than acting as the primary source of information, the students' search for knowledge is met as they learn to find answers to their questions. For students to construct knowledge, they need the opportunity to discover for themselves and practice skills in authentic situations. Providing students access to hands-on activities and allowing adequate time and space to use materials that reinforce the lesson being studied creates an opportunity for individual discovery and construction of knowledge to occur.

Equally important to self-discovery is having the opportunity to study things that are meaningful and relevant to one's life and interests. Developing a curriculum around student interests fosters intrinsic motivation and stimulates the passion to learn. One way to take learning in a direction relevant to student interest is to invite student dialogue about the lessons and

Table 18.2

units of study. Given the opportunity for input, students generate ideas and set goals that make for much richer activities than I could have created or imagined myself. When students have ownership in the curriculum, they are motivated to work hard and master the skills necessary to reach their goals.

Helping students to develop a deep love and respect for themselves, others, and their environment occurs through an open sharing of ideas and a judicious approach to discipline. When the voice of each student is heard, and environment evolves where students feel free to express themselves. Class meetings are one way to encourage such dialogue. I believe children have greater respect for their teachers, their peers, and the lessons presented when they feel safe and sure of what is expected of them. In setting fair and consistent rules initially and stating the importance of every activity, students are shown respect for their presence and time. In turn they learn to respect themselves, others, and their environment.

For myself, teaching provides an opportunity for continual learning and growth. One of my hopes as an educator is to instill a love of learning in my students, as I share my own passion for learning with them. I feel there is a need for compassionate, strong, and dedicated individuals who are excited about working with children. In our competitive society it is important for students to not only receive a solid education, but to work with someone who is aware of and sensitive to their individual needs. I am such a person and will always strive to be the best educator that I can be.

Table 18.2

Sample 2

I believe the children are our future...

I believe each and every child has the potential to bring something unique and special to the world. I will help children to develop their potential by believing in them as capable individuals. I will assist children in discovering who they are, so they can express their own opinions and nurture their own ideas. I have a vision of a world where people learn to respect, accept, and embrace the differences between us, as the core of what makes life so fascinating.

Teach them well and let them lead the way...

Every classroom presents a unique community of learners that varies not only in abilities, but also in learning styles. My role as a teacher is to give children the tools with which to cultivate their own gardens of knowledge. To accomplish this goal, I will teach to the needs of each child so that all learners can feel capable and successful. I will present curriculum that involves the interests of the children and makes learning relevant to life. I will incorporate themes, integrated units, projects, group work, individual work, and hands-on learning in order to make children active learners. Finally, I will tie learning into the world community to help children become caring and active members of society.

Show them all the beauty they possess inside.
Give them a sense of pride...

My classroom will be a caring, safe, and equitable environment where each child can blossom and grow. I will allow children to become responsible members of our classroom community by using strategies such as class meetings, positive discipline, and democratic principles. In showing children how to become responsible for themselves as well as their own learning, I am giving them the tools to become successful in life, to believe in themselves, and to love themselves.

Let the children's laughter remind us how we used to be...

Teaching is a lifelong learning process of learning about new philosophies and new strategies, learning from the parents and community, learning from colleagues, and especially learning from the children. Children have taught me to open my mind and my heart to the joys, the innocence, and the diversity of ideas in the world. Because of this, I will never forget how to smile with the new, cherish the old, and laugh with the children.

Strategy 19

Proclaim Your Student Teaching Goals

**When we are motivated by goals that have deep meaning,
by dreams that need completion, by pure love that needs
expressing, then we truly live.**

— Greg Anderson

You may be asking yourself, *"How will I know if I am successful at student teaching?"* How will you answer that? Many student teachers try to improve a hundred different things at a time to be more successful. Others simply show up and try their best each day. Then there are those who have a clear vision, based on their education philosophy, that set for themselves challenging, but attainable, goals. Which group do you think will be the most successful at student teaching?

Refer back to the education process of building a foundation of knowledge, applying that knowledge to teaching, and reflecting on how to improve. Goal setting is at the core of this ongoing process. Every teacher and student teacher should identify an area in need of improvement, set specific goals to meet that deficiency, work passionately to meet those goals, measure the results, and then begin again with another area in need of improvement. This process of goal setting, action, and evaluation should be evident in all our work from lesson planning to professional development plans.

In preparation for your student teaching, you need to *reflect on what you want to accomplish in your student teaching.* This will be different for everyone. For instance, one student teacher may want to gain the confidence to speak in front of a class without turning into a sweaty mop. Another may wish to receive a stellar recommendation and a fulltime teaching position at that school. Whatever your goals, use the valuable goal setting process to achieve them.

Be careful in goal setting! In my time in business, I quickly learned the value of goal setting to staying competitive. However, just setting goals is not the answer. In my experience, the companies that were unsuccessful and eventually went broke were the ones that:

1) Set goals without regard to their vision

2) Developed unattainable goals

3) Neglected to evaluate the effectiveness of their goals or how to improve the process

4) Failed to communicate their goals to employees

These businesses took goal setting as the end point. Their aim was not to support their vision, or improve their business, but to set goals for the sake of setting goals.

How to Set Effective Goals

Set Goals That Support Your Philosophy

As a first step in setting your goals, look at your education philosophy statement. This is your vision for how you will support your students and their learning, and for how you will manage your classroom. Your goals should align with your philosophy.

Example

In the sample philosophy statement (see Table 18.3), the Ohio State preservice teacher wrote:

"My role as a teacher is to give children the tools with which to cultivate their own gardens of knowledge. To accomplish this goal, I will teach to the needs of each child so that all learners can feel capable and successful. I will present curriculum that involves the interests of the children and makes learning relevant to life. I will incorporate themes, integrated units, projects, group work, individual work, and hands-on learning in order to make children active learners."

Based on this philosophy, a sample supportive goal could be: to implement at least one group activity and one hands-on activity using an integrated unit during student teaching.

Develop Measurable Goals That are Challenging, yet Attainable

Idealism needs to be mixed with a little realism. Too often in education, goals that are neither measurable nor attainable create rather than solve problems. If a goal cannot be measured, you will never know if you are meeting the goal, or even if you are on the right track to meet it. If the goals are not attainable, people quickly become fatigued and frustrated.

Example

The fictitious American Middle School (AMS) set a goal to improve reading scores by 70% in one year, and challenged each teacher to meet this goal. How can you – the teacher – accomplish this in your classroom? This goal is probably unattainable, unless someone develops a magical new reading program. A more suitable goal for AMS would be "through the successful implementation of the SSR (silent sustained reading) program in every classroom AMS will see 10–15% gains in reading." A 10–15% increase in reading is challenging for any school, but it is attainable.

Evaluate Your Effectiveness

Once you set goals that are measurable, challenging, attainable, and that support your philosophy, you still have to monitor and evaluate your progress in meeting those goals. Monitoring encompasses various qualitative and quantitative measures, such as observations, surveys, student work, testing, and performance evaluations.

Example

You have implemented SSR in your classroom to support the reading goal of AMS. You monitor the improvement in reading by testing a significant sample of students every four months. Evaluation involves comparing results from before and after you adopted the new program. Using this data, you can determine if the SSR program increased reading scores and by how much. Most importantly, if your data show only minimal progress in meeting the goal, you can research other best practices related to SSR, or supplementary activities in conjunction with the SSR program, to help improve the reading scores. With ongoing monitoring, you can evaluate the results and continue to adjust the program until you have reached the established reading goal.

Proclaim Your Goals

We all need encouragement and gentle reminders of what we are working towards. First, *write down your goals* and describe how you will measure them. Second, *post your goals* where you will see them every day—inside your visor in your car, on your bed stand, or taped to a mirror. In this way, you get a daily reminder of your goals. Moreover, it is extremely refreshing to cross off goals from your list as you accomplish them. Over time, you will be proud to see all that you have achieved. Last, but not least, *communicate your goals* to someone else. This person could be your cooperating teacher, your clinical supervisor, or a mentor. By putting your goals into the public domain, you are holding yourself more accountable and you are more likely to follow-up and meet those goals.

Examples of Student Teaching Goals

As you begin your student teaching, establish three to four specific goals for yourself, with monitoring and evaluation procedures. Remember that your goals should support your philosophy, be challenging yet attainable, and measurable. This is a fabulous beginning to your student teaching reflection. Reexamining your teaching philosophy and establishing your student goals certainly will not cure your anxiety about student teaching, but it will give you a strong foundation to start with and send you off in the right direction.

Table 19.1

Examples of Student Teaching Goals

Example	Implement a new instructional strategy, such as the jigsaw approach, to increase student learning.
Monitoring	Initially use the strategy for 1-2 classes. Use the other classes as a baseline to determine the effectiveness of the strategy. Use student surveys to gather the students' perspective on how the approach affected their learning.
Evaluation/ Process Improvement	Compare the results (e.g. test scores, homework results) from the baseline classes to the classes where you implemented the strategy. Determine if there is a significant difference between the two groups by analyzing student performance results. Review the student surveys. From the results and surveys, determine strengths and weaknesses. Reflect on how you can improve the implementation of this new strategy for the other classes.

Example	Increase parent involvement by 20% by, 1) creating at least two new opportunities for their involvement, and 2) sending a parent letter encouraging them to participate.
Monitoring	Create a baseline of current parent involvement and the number of opportunities they have to be involved inside and outside the classroom.
Evaluation/ Process Improvement	Compare the baseline to the parents' involvement and number of opportunities available after the initiative. Determine how much the parent involvement increased after the initiative. Reflect on how the parent involvement affected the student learning. Brainstorm on how the goal could be further supported, e.g., broadening the modes of communication and/or increasing opportunities for involvement.

Example	Improve classroom behavior by using an engaging, high-interest curriculum.
Monitoring	Develop a baseline of how many discipline referrals (parent and administration) were issued in the past month, quarter, and semester.
Evaluation/ Process Improvement	Compare the baseline to the number of issued referrals after the introduction of the new curriculum. Reflect on the impact the curriculum had on student learning and the reduction of disruptive behavior. Devise ways to apply this approach in other classes and throughout the school year.

Strategy 20

Research the School and Students

What is research but a blind date with knowledge?

— Will Harvey

You have completed the first two steps in student teaching: creating a philosophy statement and establishing goals. By now you know where you will be doing your student teaching, and with whom. The third step in preparing for a successful student teaching experience is to research and learn about your new school and its students. Chances are you have never been in the school, nor have you met any of the students. If you have, through work experience or just by visiting, then you are ahead of the game, and the first day of student teaching will not feel so much like a blind date. Nonetheless, further research of your student teaching assignment is critical. By gathering information on the school you can familiarize yourself with the students and their backgrounds, the school and its goals, the classrooms and classes offered, and the school community. Knowing this information prior to student teaching can alleviate some of the anxiety every student teacher suffers.

To learn about the school, talk to teachers that teach or used to teach there. Use the Internet to visit the websites of the school, the district, and the state education office. Watch for and clip articles from the local newspaper about the school. Call the local Chamber of Commerce and ask for community and school information.

Following are questions to guide you in your research. For more resources and questions to guide your research, see Strategy 46.

School Research Questions

- What is the student make-up of the school (special education, bilingual, ethnic backgrounds, income)?

- What types of learning initiatives are in place at the school?

- What are the school's test scores? How are those scores trending? What are areas of strength and weakness? (This information can usually be found on the state education office website.)

- What is the typical class size?

- How many students and teachers are there?

- What kind of curricula and programs does the school offer?

- Where is the school located?

- What are the school guidelines, school rules, and emergency procedures?

- Who are the key players (principals, department heads, etc), and what are their backgrounds?

- What are the community's (positive and/or negative) impressions of the school?

In performing due diligence on your student teaching assignment, you reduce the anxiety surrounding the student teacher experience, and you develop a greater understanding of your students and their learning needs. Overall, you position yourself for a successful student teaching experience.

Strategy 21

Keep Abreast of Your Field

We now accept the fact that learning is a lifelong process of keeping abreast of change. And the most pressing task is to teach people how to learn.

— Peter F. Drucker

In addition to learning about the school, you should study the latest best practices in research and pedagogy. You can keep abreast of changes by joining general education and content-specific organizations, and by perusing educational journals and websites. These resources can provide you with curriculum ideas, connections to experts, publications, conferences, e-workshops, and job banks.

Professional Education Organizations

Phi Delta Kappa (PDK) (www.pdkintl.org) offers a valuable free service to all preservice and new teachers (both members and non-members): the *Teacher to Teacher E-Mentoring* program. This "national electronic mentoring initiative [is] designed to help beginning teachers overcome the challenges they face in their first years by connecting them with veteran educators via technology." If you have a question, you can email a veteran teacher (at teacherconnection@pdkintl.org) for their support and advice—anonymously, if you prefer. You can also view questions posed by other new teachers, along with the veteran teachers' responses.

I joined Phi Delta Kappa (PDK) during my preservice training. I have been a member ever since and am now involved in my local chapter. In my opinion, the benefits outweigh the cost of joining. Here are some benefits that you enjoy when you are a member:

- Grants and scholarships
- Conferences and events
- International travel
- Training opportunities
- Numerous publications (including searchable archives)
- Access to the latest research

When I joined the local chapter, I also joined a strong support group of veteran teachers who answered all my teaching and classroom questions, suggested new ideas and instructional strategies, and provided insights into the job market. I enjoy reading the PDK publications, which cover diverse educational topics and are supported by a wealth of research. Their publications cover topics ranging from overall trends in education to helpful, practical tips for classroom management. My involvement with this professional education organization has had a significant and direct impact on my professional growth and my students' learning.

Another great service for preservice and regular teachers is ProTeacher® (PT) Community (www.proteacher.net). At the PT website, new teachers can post questions and concerns that veteran teachers respond to. In addition, you can search their archives for tested lesson plans, best-practice instructional strategies, and tips for the classroom.

On the following pages, is a list of education organizations that focus on specific content areas. Find your area of concentration and visit the organization's website to explore their teacher resources and tools.

Table 21.1

Area of Concentration	Name of Professional	Association Website
Art	National Art Education Association	www.naea-reston.org
Bilingual	National Association for Bilingual and Multicultural Education	www.nabe.org
Business	Association for Career and Technical Education	www.acteonline.org
Early Childhood	National Association for the Education of Young Children	www.naeyc.org
Economics	National Council on Economic Education	www.ncee.net
English/Language Arts	National Council of Teachers of English	www.ncte.org
Foreign Languages	American Council on the Teaching of Foreign Languages	www.actfl.org
Geography	National Council for Geographic Education	www.ncge.org
Health	American Association for Health Education	www.aahperd.org/aahe
Information Technology	Association for the Advancement of Computing in Education	www.aace.org
Library	American Library Association	www.ala.org
Math	National Council for Teachers of Math	www.nctm.org
Middle School	National Middle School Association	www.nmsa.org
Music	Music Teachers National Association	www.mtna.org
Physical Education	National Association for Sports and Physical Education	www.aahperd.org/naspe/
Psychology	Teachers of Psychology in Secondary Schools	www.apa.org/ed/topsshomepage.html
Reading	International Reading Association	www.reading.org
Science	National Science Teachers Association	www.nsta.org
Social Studies	National Council for the Social Studies	www.ncss.org

Table 21.1

Area of Concentration	Name of Professional	Association Website
Special Education: Exceptional Children	Council for Exceptional Children	www.cec.sped.org
Special Education: Gifted Children	American Association for Gifted Children	www.aagc.org
Technology	Association for Education Communications and Technology	www.aect.org

Education Research Websites

Reading education journals will expose you to many creative ideas and new best practices that could be useful in your classroom. Education World® provides a wonderful platform from which to search for articles on education, instruction strategies, and general tips on almost any topic related to teaching. Its website is www.education-world.com.

Education Resources Information Center (ERIC), supported by the Department of Education, is the world's premier database of journal and non-journal education literature, with nearly 1.2 million citations dating back to 1966. This site also provides access to 110,000 full-text materials at no charge. ERIC's website is www.eric.ed.gov. This is an ideal place to begin research on almost any education topic. Use these web resources as a springboard to implement new best practices in your own classroom to improve student learning.

Strategy 22

Communicate Early With Your Cooperating Teacher

A smile is the universal welcome.

— Max Eastman

There is no reason to wait until the first day of student teaching to build a relationship with your cooperating teacher and new students. Before that day comes, you can try to get contact information for your cooperating teacher and call to set up an informal meeting, or a time for you to observe the classroom. Getting acquainted with the teacher, students, and school before you begin student teaching is a proactive step towards a positive student teaching experience.

Here are some helpful tips for the first meeting with your cooperating teacher and/or observing the classroom:

- *Dress professionally* because first impressions count. It is usually better to be a little overdressed than underdressed. For men, a nice dress shirt with a tie and dress slacks would be appropriate. Even if you know the school's culture is extremely casual in dress wear the tie anyway. You can always take it off later. For women, a nice blouse with dress slacks or skirt is fine.

- *Ask the teacher to introduce you to the classroom and explain why you are there.* Although the cooperating teacher will often introduce the student teacher, some will ask you to introduce yourself. Before you head off for your meeting prepare a brief 20 second introduction of yourself. Then practice your delivery. This will alleviate the stress of being put on the spot.

- *Observe the teacher and the classroom environment closely, and take notes for future reference.* Is there anything that strikes you about the instruction or classroom environment?

- *Smile and interact with the students.* Avoid being a fly on the wall. Since these are the same students you will soon be teaching, spend some time establishing a rapport with them. But, do not become a distraction while the cooperating teacher is teaching a lesson. The best time to approach students is when they are doing individual or group work.

- *Develop a sense of what the students have learned* and what they are currently learning. If you can find some time to talk to the cooperating teacher, ask what the students are studying and what you will most likely be teaching. If the students routinely use a classroom textbook, ask to borrow one. This information will help you in lesson planning.

- *Most importantly, express your sincere enthusiasm and gratitude* about working with the cooperating teacher and the students. Everybody loves a little praise, so compliment the cooperating teacher on something you observed, whether it is the classroom setup, the behavior of the students, or an instructional strategy used.

- *Ask the cooperating teacher if it is okay to contact him or her in the future* with further questions or to request feedback on lesson plans, and what is the best way to do so.

- *Share your student teaching goals* and express some of your worries. Remember that your cooperating teacher was once a student teacher preparing for the first day in the classroom.

Strategy 23

Begin Lesson Planning Early

**If you think it's expensive to hire a professional to do the job,
wait until you hire an amateur.**

— Red Adair

A preservice teacher is an amateur teacher — one who lacks some of the skills of a professional teacher. An amateur becomes a professional through practice — and lots of it. Your practice begins with student teaching, especially for lesson planning.

If you have spoken to your cooperating teacher, you should have a good sense of what topics, lessons, and/or units you will be teaching. Granted, you probably do not have all the answers and countless variables are still floating around in your head. But, even if you only have some sliver of an idea of what you are going to teach, start lesson planning immediately.

When writing your lesson plan, go back to your student teaching goals (see Strategy 19). What do you want to accomplish? Delivering high interest, hands-on curriculum? Using a new best-practice instructional strategy? Whatever your goals are, try to incorporate them into your lesson planning. Begin by establishing student learning outcomes. Then determine how you will assess that outcome. Finally, develop your plan to teach the students and achieve that outcome. Remember to have fun and be creative.

The truth is, you may or may not use these exact lesson plans when you begin student teaching. Your cooperating teacher may ask you to modify your lessons to fit with his or her desired outcomes. Before you begin student teaching share some of the lesson plans with your cooperating teacher and ask for feedback. Even if you have to redo all or part of them, practice in lesson planning is a valuable exercise in preparing for student teaching.

Strategy 24

- - - - - - - - - - - -

Get Your Feet Wet Early On

**To do anything truly worth doing, I must not stand back shivering
and thinking of the cold and danger, but jump in with gusto
and scramble through as well as I can.**

— Og Mandino

Student teaching bridges the gap between teacher training and the real
classroom. You may not feel ready to teach, but, at this stage, the best
advice is to jump in headfirst and be an active participant in the classroom.
This does not mean that you should teach a lesson on your first day. Yet,
within your first few days you should take small steps to playing a more
active role in the classroom.

There are easy ways to take on an active role, short of teaching a lesson.
Take attendance for the classroom. Your cooperating teacher will undoubtedly
be delighted if you take on this task because it can feel like an unpleasant chore
when done every day for years. You can turn this dull task into an opportunity
to learn the students' names by making it into a game. Each time you take
attendance give yourself a point for each student's name you remember. Keep
a tally as you work towards your goal: to achieve a 100% score in remembering
all the students' names. Another way is to help teach part of a lesson.

> On my second day of student teaching, the cooperating teacher
> put me charge of the geography review quiz for approximately
> 15 minutes at the end of the period. I was nervous, as this was
> my first time in the role of teacher. Fortunately, my cooperating

teacher made the transition easy. She gave the lesson for the first two periods, and then handed it over to me for the remaining classes. Once I started, I had a lot of fun; it was a great way to get in front of the students without feeling any "teacher pressure." It also helped ease some of my anxiety and prepared me for teaching entire lessons.

Create an active presence in the classroom. Move around the classroom and initiate positive interactions with the students. The students are watching you. When you are active – walking around the room, observing, assessing, and giving feedback – you show them that you are confident in yourself and your abilities. You are letting them know that you are ready for this role, and you will be good at it. If you sit in the corner like a lump on a log, the students will see you as insecure and not up to the job, which will make it all that harder for you when you start teaching them.

Lastly, take some responsibility for grading. Of course, you should ask for both permission and instructions from the cooperating teacher before you begin grading the students' work. To ensure fairness in assessment, the teacher probably uses a rubric, an answer sheet, or a baseline when grading, so you should use the same tools. Also, with grading comes the responsibility to give your students effective feedback. Student teachers should provide feedback that is clear, specific, and related to the lesson objectives. Whenever possible, it should be directly connected to student concerns. In College Knowledge, David T. Conley (2005) writes:

> "All feedback should help students understand the key skills they need to be developing, not just what they get right or wrong. The feedback should be complex and detailed. Feedback on writing, for example, should critique overall organization, quality of argumentation, originality of thought, and accuracy of assertions, in addition to conventions and use of language. Feedback in science labs should focus on the degree to which students demonstrate understanding of scientific principles or the quality of their explanations of observed phenomena, in addition to how well

they conduct an experiment. Feedback in math should focus on methods of problem solving, nontraditional solutions to problems, and student understanding of underlying mathematical concepts, in addition to number of correct answers. This is not to say that correct answers should not be valued, but only that the underlying cognitive processes necessary to construct them should be considered equally important."

Strategy 25

- - - - - - - - - - - -

Learn Names Quickly

Remember that a person's name is to that person the sweetest and most important sound in any language.

— Dale Carnegie

There is a significant payoff in learning the names of students and staff as soon as you can. Learning someone's name is an important step in building a positive relationship and rapport with that person. The absence of a rapport with your students creates a significant barrier to effective classroom management.

Learning names can be challenging. In the first few weeks of the school year, teachers are bombarded with new names and faces: students, teachers, support staff, administration, parents, and the list goes on. At first, it is hard to retain all these new names (often well over 100 in any year), but, with an applied effort, over time you will be able to remember the vast majority. There are some easy steps you can take to foster a positive rapport with students and staff.

Repetition is a great learning aid. Make a point of greeting your students by name when they enter the classroom or when you see them in the hallway. If a student you don't know or remember comes into the classroom, politely ask them to remind you of their name. Alternatively, make note of where that student sits and refer to your seating chart. Undoubtedly, you will sometimes call a student by the wrong name. And from time to time students will attempt to exploit the fact that you don't know all their names. Do not get discouraged; move past all your mistakes. In time, you will learn all their names. By doing so, you will develop a closer, more positive relationship with your students. You will quickly notice that the students will respond better when they know you KNOW who they are. Simply put, it is important to the students and they will appreciate your effort to get to know them.

A seating chart is a simple, but critical tool that will help you to remember your students' names. You will need one for each of your classes. To save time ask your cooperating teacher for a copy or spare seating chart. If the cooperating teacher does not have a seating chart, create your own. The simplest way to do this is draw one out on regular paper, writing in the students' names. You can create a more sophisticated seating chart with few 8X11 metal sheets and some small magnets, readily available at your local education supply store or on the Internet. Put a white label with the students name on each magnet and arrange each magnet to show where the students are seated in the class. This chart can be easily modified if your students change seats.

In your first few weeks keep the seating chart with you at all times (when grading, lecturing, etc.) When calling on the students use the seating chart to help remember students' names or to call on the students that you frequently overlook. You should aim to call on every student at least once every week.

> One mental exercise I found effective is to picture a student, try to recall his or her name, and then confirm it with the seating chart. If I were correct then I would make it a point to talk to that student using their name as much as possible. I found that this repetition really helped me remember their names.

A note of caution—if you are stuck on a student's name, avoid saying "hey you" to get the student's attention. While this can be a natural way of getting the attention of someone, in the classroom it suggests that you do not value that student's individuality. If you are being observed by your clinical supervisor or your cooperating teacher and you shout out a few "hey you's" this will certainly be reflected in your student teacher evaluation.

The effort to build rapport by learning names should extend outside your classroom. Begin by learning the names of your principal, assistant principals, team teachers, aides, parents, and volunteers. Eventually, widen your circle to include other teachers, custodians, and office support staff. Not only is this is a professional courtesy, you are also more likely to receive needed help when you know the name of the person of whom you are asking a favor. Z

Strategy 26

Impress Through Your Teaching

There's a roughness and a surprising nature to most B movies that you don't get in classic films—something more immediate. I never chose those movies to leave impressions in my brain, they just did.

— Tim Burton

Doing an outstanding job student teaching is important because you are being graded and this is your time to practice, right? Sure, but student teaching is also a vital step before landing your dream teaching job. To take the "right step" and not a "misstep" in student teaching boils downs to making a unique and positive impression through your teaching.

If you are interested in teaching at the school where you are student teaching keep in mind that principals often prefer to hire people they know and whose teaching abilities they trust. Therefore, you should go that extra mile to ensure that the principal hears only positive feedback about you. This is your time to stand out from the rest of the student teachers that have marched through the same halls.

How do you stand out? Consider Tim Burton's quote about B movies at the beginning of this section. B movies, by definition, are not highly polished, but it is that unfinished quality and the surprises they often contain that leave an impression. You do not have to be the A+ preservice teacher to get great results and make a great impression. You do have to put your all effort into producing and delivering an energetic, high-interest, standard-based curriculum in a fair, respectful classroom. Push yourself to be an innovator, a researcher of new ideas and best practices, and a calculated risk taker. In the end, you may find that you have left your mark and facilitated many unanticipated and affirmative learning outcomes for your students.

Lesson Planning and Instructional Strategies

Think for a moment about your favorite teacher. Why was this person effective in teaching? Was your favorite teacher's methodology solely lectures, movies, and worksheets? Unless the teacher was a master at lecturing (and a few teachers are), it is more likely that your favorite teacher used a variety of instructional strategies to reach all the diverse learners in the classroom. Your favorite teacher may also have leavened methodology with a little humor and humility and presented it in a way that was both engaging and meaningful to your life. Think of your favorite teacher when designing your lesson plans. Then ask yourself these questions?

- Does the lesson have a clear and understandable learning objective that has been communicated to the students?

- Have I *connected* the learning objective to the *students' lives* and made it meaningful?

- Do I use a *variety of methodologies* to reach most of the diverse learners in the classroom? See Table 26.1 for a comprehensive list of strategies and techniques.

- Do I offer *alternative assessments* to evaluate the students' learning?

- What is an *idea* that I can implement to make this an *impressionable* learning experience for the student?

Example

While a student teacher at a middle school I gave a lesson on poverty for the Social Studies class. Most of the students in the school were from middle-class families. After a few weeks of student teaching, I had observed that many were apathetic about anyone outside their own world, which, for a middle-school student, would typically consist of friends, teachers, and family. For most of these students, poverty simply did not exist. In the first few lessons, I planned for the students to explore the definition of poverty and "feel" the magnitude of the poverty problem.

I knew that for the lesson to be significant and impact the students it had to be surprising and authentic. For a week, I

Table 26.1

Strategies and Techniques to
Meet Students' Diverse Learning Needs

Building Background	Interaction	Strategies	Practice/ Assessment
Student experiences	Cooperative learning	Teacher modeling	Reflective writing
K-W-L chart	Peer tutoring	Timelines	Story summary
Vocabulary book	Learning stations	Flow charts	Wonder ball
Freyer model	Jigsawing	Mapping	Experiments
Brainstorming	Interviewing	Charting	Character diaries
Semantic webbing	Games	Graphing	Outcome sentences
Maps, photos, illustrations, and primary sources	Socratic Seminars	Venn diagram	Exit slips
	Group narratives	Art / music / dance	Role play
Bell notes	Think – pair – share	Hands-on / field trip	Strip story
Small group discussion			

brainstormed, reviewed the cooperating teacher's materials, and researched resources on the Internet. Finally, I began to construct the unit. On the first day, I went into the classroom and stacked 26 of the 30 desks on top of each other, so no student could use them. When the first period began the first four students to arrive sat at the four desks with chairs in the classroom. These four students represented the percentage of the rich in the world. I had ten students just sit on chairs for the lesson. These students represented the middle class. The other 14–16 students sat on the floor with nothing—representing the poor of the world.

Immediately the students were asking,

"Mr. Hougan, why do I need to sit on the floor?"

"Mr. Hougan, are you crazy?"

"What are we learning about?"

Others caught on by asking, "This is about our new unit on poverty, right?"

From the first moment they walked in the door, the students were plugged in and ready to learn about poverty. When the bell rang, signaling the start of the period, I asked the students to work on their anticipatory question, "How does the current seating arrangement relate to poverty?" After a few minutes of writing, we dove into a class discussion about global poverty. In a brainstorming session, the students figured out that the desks and chairs reflected the percentages of rich, middle class, and poor in the world. I ended the discussion by affirming that the students were right and reviewed the lesson's learning objectives. Next, the students explored the meaning of poverty from different perspectives. Ten students read narratives of people all around the world living in poverty. After 20 minutes of the descriptive narratives, and sitting on the uncomfortable floor many of the students "felt" the lesson. A few students were even misty eyed. The students partnered up to discuss what they learned. They were asked to write down conditions that may lead to poverty and where poverty is most prevalent. Finally, we had a whole group discussion and wrote down their responses. Right before class ended Tyler (the class instigator) stood up and said that we should do something about this.

"Great idea Tyler! How would the class feel about doing some project to help poverty? Would you help me, Tyler, to create the project guidelines?"

I had already planned some type of community activity relating to poverty, but there was no way that I was going to let the students know that. During lunch period, over the next few days, Tyler and I developed the unit's assessment, which included reflections, research, and a local community activity.

This opening lesson definitely left an impression. All day the students were talking about what they learned and how much fun they had doing it. The students did not only talk to other students, but to teachers and staff. A few hours after my first period class, teachers, and administration were popping into the classroom to see what all the chatter was about. They loved the lesson too. This favorable impression helped me immensely when I requested recommendation letters for my job search.

Strategy 27

- - - - - - - - - - - -

Use Classroom Management to Your Advantage

It's hard to be fully creative without structure and constraint. Try to paint without a canvas. Creativity and freedom are two sides of the same coin. I like the best of both worlds. Want freedom? Get organized. Want to get organized? Get creative.

— David Allen

Most student teachers have two matters of concern: classroom management and discipline. Their anxiety mainly stems from inexperience and a lack of understanding of how to apply classroom management in the classroom. A thorough examination of classroom management is outside the scope of this book. However, this section will offer several quick and easy classroom management techniques that may be implemented at any grade-level.

Classroom management is a system of practices that increases learning and lowers behavioral problems. Effective classroom management communicates your expectations to the students. As a student teacher, you will need to work with the cooperating teacher's classroom management style. However, if you identify some classroom problems that interfere with the students' learning, then you can try various classroom management techniques to address the problem.

Bell/Anticipatory Notes

One classroom management technique, applicable to K-12 grades, includes an exercise called "bell notes," also known as anticipatory notes or entry tasks. Bell notes are straightforward and effective. Every day, students are required to write into their journals the answers to a question or statement written on the classroom whiteboard. This simple technique has many benefits: it provides a consistent routine, so the students know what is expected of them from the minute they walk into the classroom; it reduces student misbehavior; and, it shortens the time it takes to start a class. The bell note gets the students thinking from the onset of class. Bell notes can spur students' interest in the day's lesson or incite them to review information from previous lessons. They also build on the students' background by connecting to the their lives and their existing body of knowledge.

Last, but not least, the teacher can do come administrative tasks, such as taking attendance, while the students complete their bell notes. This eliminates class downtime, which increases learning time for the students. Assume that a teacher working in a 180-day school uses bellnotes and reduces downtime by four minutes a day. This translates to an additional 12 hours of learning time for the students in a year. Using meaningful bell notes in a consistent manner will lead to improved student learning and will reflect positively in your student teaching evaluations.

Question and Concern Box

A question and concern box can also be an effective tool for classroom management. It gives students a way to express questions that may seem pressing to them, but in a way that does not disrupt the flow of the lesson and class.

> I remember the frustration I felt in my first few weeks of teaching, when students would interrupt a class discussion, or my instructions, with questions not relevant to the topic of discussion. The students' questions ranged from, "What is my grade in the class?" to "What homework do I need to make-up?"
>
> These are valid questions, but they are not appropriate for classroom instruction or discussion time. Ultimately, the students' untimely questions reduced instruction time, detracted from meaningful class discussions, and negatively impacted the students' learning. To remedy this situation, I explained to the students that their questions and concerns were valid, but they would be handled with a question and concern box. I asked

the students to please write notes to me with their questions or concerns, place them in the box, and I would respond within twenty-four hours (for middle school students writing a note was going to be no problem).

Amazingly, this idea worked! I received about 5-6 notes a day, fewer students derailed group discussions with irrelevant questions, and class discussion flowed more freely. In addition, the students liked the personal feedback I was able to provide rather than the rushed response I would give them during class time. In the beginning, students would forget to put their names on their notes, but a few reminders solved that problem.

Managing the Paperwork

Student teachers often struggle to return graded papers. The amount of paperwork to be checked and properly graded can be overwhelming, even without trying to provide high-quality feedback on the students' work (see Strategy 24). Most student teachers do not have a plan for returning students' work, and countless reasons from fire drills to exciting lessons can delay the return of student work with the all-important teacher feedback. Research shows that feedback is more effective when delivered in a timely fashion, so a plan for grading and returning your students' work is important.

At first, I had no classroom management plan for passing back papers. I would simply return the students' work whenever I had the chance, a cumbersome process that took away from class time. I soon realized that I had to think of some other way to do this. It dawned on me that in every period I had a few high-energy students that continually misbehaved. Why not have those students pass out the papers at the beginning of each period? Not only would the students burn off some of that energy, but they also would become a valuable part of the class. I approached the students privately and expressed my need for their help. They were intrigued by the thought that a teacher needed help and jumped at the chance to help me. These student helpers began to participate more in class and their misbehavior decreased. And my students' work with my notes and feedback were delivered in a timely and consistent manner.

Maximize Class Time

Nothing invites chaos like completing your next lesson plan 5-10 minutes before the dismissal bell rings—thus creating downtime for the students. Devoting insufficient time to lesson planning is one of the biggest mistakes teachers make, and this lack of planning may quickly lead to student misbehavior. While you are distracted, mischievous children begin to move towards the door, others may begin play fighting, and others will put their heads down. With some planning, you can turn this downtime into rich instructional and evaluative time.

Sometimes a lesson will proceed more quickly than you had anticipated, so always over plan your lessons for the day. A good rule of thumb is to plan for 10-15 minutes more than the class period allows. Or, plan a backup activity that connects to your lesson's objectives, and have this it readily available for such emergencies.

You can also use the remaining minutes of a class to reflect on and evaluate the lesson. One good technique is the use of exit slips. Review the lesson's objectives and ask the students to complete a brief self-evaluation on whether they feel they have met the stated objectives. Alternatively, the students can summarize their learning or pose clarifying questions that you can address the following day. As the students leave the classroom, the students hand you their feedback, allowing you to assess the students' learning.

Outcome sentences are another useful strategy for evaluating lessons and eliminating downtime at the end of a lesson. For this strategy, the teacher prepares various outcome sentences that are posted on the wall with a poster or an overhead projector. The teacher asks the students to write down and then state an outcome sentence (in partners, small groups, or the whole class): "I learned…", "I was surprised…", "I wonder…", I think…". This quick and engaging activity allows students to think about their learning and share it with others. From the teacher's perspective, outcome sentences serve as an insightful evaluation tool to check students' understanding of the lesson.

Consistency

Consistency is a common and critical thread in effective classroom management. In spite of slow or unexpected results, keep using your chosen techniques and monitoring your progress. If the results are unsatisfactory, then try adjusting your technique rather than abandoning it. When I started my student teaching I saw the value of using the bell note, but I also knew the practice could be improved.

What I observed in my first two weeks of student teaching was that very few students consistently completed their bell notes. Moreover, the students who did complete the bell note did so in a matter of a minute without giving serious thought to the question or statement—indicating that the students did not see much value in the practice. My goal was to make the bell note more relevant and meaningful, and encourage a higher level of completion.

I made a conscious effort to write bell notes that were more introspective, reflective, and thought provoking for the students. Furthermore, I used the bell note to connect the lesson to the students' personal lives. For instance, I would routinely ask the students to relate a personal experience to what we were learning in class. Very early on, I was encouraged to see the students writing for longer than a minute. That was the trick: connect the lesson to the student's lives. I quickly discovered that they love writing about themselves.

I then told each class that I had noticed a lot of students not completing their bell notes and that I was afraid that they were missing out on learning. Because of that, I told them that I would check their bell notes randomly as we went along, rather than just at the end of the unit. Over the next few weeks, I routinely collected the bell notes as an "exit slip." The students had to hand me their bell note in order to leave the room. The students were floored. The first day I did this only about half had completed the bell note. The remaining students scrambled to complete theirs as they were leaving. The next day I did the exact same thing. Surprisingly, about 70% of the students completed the bellnote.

I repeated this process until 90% of students were completing their bell notes at the beginning of class.

A key part of classroom management is communicating your expectations. Some students were writing their bell note quickly, to finish it, but it was junk. I told the students that I expected high quality work from my students. Their bell notes were to be thoughtful and in complete sentences.

Implementing this expectation initially caused chaos. Remember, I would collect their bell notes as exit slips at the classroom door. Thirty students are eagerly trying to escape the classroom and thirty more are eagerly trying to enter. I made it a point to glance over each bell note. I returned about a quarter that did not meet my expectations. Relentlessly, I repeatedly emphasized my belief they could do better work and were capable of providing a more thorough response. The students were upset at having to return to their seat and write a more complete, thoughtful response. Sure, there was a ton of chaos at the door, but after about a week the students knew exactly what their job was: 1) to complete their bell note when they entered the classroom, and 2) to provide thoughtful, articulate responses. Over time, I reduced my random checks. This classroom management technique had created structure, provided learning exercises that could connect to the students' lives, and communicated the expectation of high quality work.

When preparing for student teaching, you must think about how to handle the various day-to-day classroom tasks. For instance, when and how will you hand back papers? How will you take attendance? How will you manage make-up work? Your classroom management techniques should be tailored to you and your students. You will be successful in your classroom management if it involves problem solving, experimentation, consistency, and fairness.

Strategy 28

Know Yourself When it Comes to Discipline

Know thyself.

— Scribes of Dephi, via Plato

Classroom discipline is another broad topic that cannot be thoroughly examined in a book of this size. Nonetheless, the subject needs to be addressed because it is on the mind of practically every student teacher. Student teachers know that at some point, no matter how great a teacher you may be, a discipline problem will arise.

Because you will inevitably face a discipline challenge, how you deal with it is critical to your professional growth as a teacher. To establish a successful discipline policy (described further in Strategy 29), you need a framework to work within. Construct this discipline framework by reflecting on your discipline philosophy, and knowing the school rules, policies, and procedures.

Reflect on Your Discipline Philosophy

Begin by reviewing your education philosophy statement and asking yourself these questions:

- What values in your education philosophy translate into your beliefs about discipline?

- Does your discipline philosophy include such values as fairness, dignity, and equity?

- Using five adjectives, how would you describe your classroom discipline philosophy?

Jot down your ideas and begin drafting your discipline philosophy. While you are doing this exercise, ask yourself if you are going to be democratic, authoritarian, or moderate in your discipline approach. This discipline philosophy will allow you to build on your strengths and beliefs to maintain order in your classroom. For example, if you are by nature laid-back and you desire a democratic approach to classroom management and discipline, then taking on the role as an authoritarian will be exhausting and self-defeating. Since you will probably not be able to maintain that authoritarian mask, the students may hear the authoritarian verbal tone but receive a very different message from your non-verbal cues. The authors of <u>Discipline with Dignity</u> wrote, "Mixed signals often lead to agitation and anxiety in students, particularly those who are already sensitive to mixed messages. Mixed signals often culminate in conflict, confusion, and classroom management problems (Curwin & Mender, 1993)." Mixed signals, and the classroom misbehavior that result, can be avoided by establishing a classroom discipline philosophy and approach that is consistent with who you are. And this is accomplished through on-going self-reflection.

Know the School Rules, Policies, and Procedures

A second and relatively easy step to take to ease your discipline anxiety is to know the rules, policies, and procedures of the school. The more information you have, the more empowered you will be. For instance, imagine you see a student in the hallway with a red bandana hanging from their left pocket, and you sense this is somehow gang related. You do not know the student, but he is walking directly towards you. In a situation like this, do you have the necessary understanding of school rules and procedures to address the issue of gang attire?

> During my first year of teaching, I saw a student at his locker with a baseball bat. I wondered about this, since it was only second period and baseball practice was in the afternoon. So, I went over to him and asked why he had a bat. The student told me to "back off" and wondered why "teachers were all over his shit," then said that the bat was for baseball practice. I calmly stated that school policy did not allow students to have bats in the hallways or classrooms, and then asked him to turn the bat over to me.

The student responded with hostility. I restated that bats were not allowed in the hallway and told him he could recover his bat, at the end of the day, from the front office. The student responded with increased hostility. I asked him to walk with me to the front office and speak with school administration about the matter. Meanwhile, I signaled to a passing teacher to call security. The student expressed his intention to carry his bat to class. I gave him some space and followed him at a safe distance down the hallway. Fortunately, security and administration caught up with him before he made it to his scheduled class. Administration staff later informed me that the student had a behavior disorder and held a grudge with one of the students in his next class. Because I knew the school policy – that bats were considered weapons – I was empowered to intervene, and my intervention, while a little tense for me, may well have prevented a serious incident.

Begin your research by combing the school's handbook to become familiar with its stated policies. Many schools have electronic versions of their handbooks posted on their websites. If you cannot locate one online then ask your cooperating teacher or school administration for a copy. The handbook is a valuable resource for information on schedules, mission and belief statements, staff contacts, technology and emergency guidelines, as well as discipline. It should provide a sufficient explanation of school policies on:

- Drugs
- Alcohol
- Weapons
- Insubordination
- Offenses against property
- Indecency

- Physical and verbal abuse
- Classroom infractions
- Misbehavior off-campus
- Tardiness and absences
- Dress regulations
- Due process

Learning the school's policies and procedures on student discipline creates the necessary framework for your decision-making on discipline in your classroom.

Strategy 29

Establish and Enforce Expectations
for Classroom Behavior

Do I have to know rules and all that crap? Then forget it.

— John Daly

By now, you should have shaped your classroom management and discipline philosophy. In addition, you have studied and become familiar with the school policies on discipline to create a framework for effective decision-making. The logical next step is to create an outline of your expectations for classroom behavior. There are two approaches to laying out the classroom expectations/rules.

Traditional Approach to Classroom Rules

The first approach is the more traditional approach. You think of your non-negotiable rules, e.g., no food in class, no late homework, do not interrupt others, do not be late, respect your peers or teachers. Of course, the list can go on and on, so pick no more than five or six. Once you know what these are, reframe them as positive outcomes, rather than prohibitions (see the examples on the opposite page).

This traditional approach works best with elementary and middle school students as it explicitly states the behavior expectations for each day. It is important that you discuss these rules, stress the importance of following them, and visibly post them throughout the classroom.

One twist to this traditional approach is to develop the classroom rules with all the students and create a social contract, rather then using the more authoritarian approach where the teacher dictates the rules.

Table 29.1

Establish Positive Classroom Rules

Negative	Positive
No food in class	Leave your food in the cafeteria
No late homework	Turn in your homework on time
Don't interrupt others	Please wait your turn to speak
Don't be late	Be in your seat and working at the bell
Don't be disrespectful	Respect yourself, peers, and teachers.

Expectations Approach to Classroom Rules

High school students may require a different approach. Imagine for a moment that you are a high school student. You have six or seven teachers in a day. More than likely each teacher has his or her own set of classroom rules. You review all the teachers' rules and you realize one teacher says it okay to have food in the classroom, while another does not. Some teachers allow headsets, and others do not. Some tolerate small talk, and others do not. If you are in a traditional high school, you will be switching classrooms with all these different rules and norms every 45-55 minutes. At the beginning of each semester, you may get a few new teachers with new rules. Repeat this process for another three years. Are you frustrated yet?

What I call the "Expectations Approach" is slightly different. The teacher lays out 3-4 simple expectations, and together the teacher and the students define these expectations and provide examples of how to meet them. The students, as individuals and/or small groups, then create a short list of classroom rules that support these expectations.

How to Implement the Expectations Approach

The teacher begins with a list of non-negotiable behavior expectations, then reduces the list to the top three. When creating your expectations it is best to keep the expectations to one word. For instance, in my classroom I expect the students to be *productive, professional,* and *respectful.* Then I provide the students a worksheet that looks like this:

Table 29.2

Expectations	Productive	Professional	Respectful
Definition			
Examples			
List classroom rules that support the expectations			

The students work individually or in small groups to develop definitions, examples, and classroom rules that support the classroom expectations, which are then shared with the entire class. It is important to connect expectations to the classroom rules the students have already encountered in their school years. For instance, under what expectation category would you place the classroom rule, "Be on time to class?" Most students list it under being professional. How about the classroom rule "Make your best effort to complete in-class activities?" This rule would support the expectation of being productive. How about the classroom rule "Keep your hands and feet to yourself?" Students usually list this rule as supporting the expectation of being respectful or even perhaps professional.

As a follow-up activity, the teacher can give a pop quiz the next day asking the students to list the three classroom expectations classroom and describe one classroom rule that supports each of those expectations. The teacher should quickly identify and work with any student that cannot demonstrate their understanding of the class expectations, through an individual student conference or by calling the student at home. A swift response will clearly communicate that you expect students to meet the class expectations and will help prevent future misunderstandings.

This approach groups all of the classroom rules needed to run a class smoothly under three to four categories that together comprise your expectations for classroom behavior. The students no longer have to memorize lists, or try to remember which teacher has what rules. Instead, they have a framework for how to behave in the classroom. High school students have expressed their preference for this approach because they are not being directly told what or what not to do. Instead, the young scholars feel they are being treated more like adults and professional students.

Reinforce the Behavior Expectations Through Clear Rewards and Consequences

Once you chose the appropriate approach to developing your classroom rules and expectations you need to clearly communicate the rewards and consequences for following or breaking them. This is an ongoing process, not a one-time event at the beginning of the year. Remember that it is as important to have rewards for good behavior as it is to have consequences for bad behavior. Here are some ideas for rewards that other teachers and I have used:

- Call home. This is a great way to develop a positive relationship with the parent and the student. Many times the parent or students cringe when they get a call from the school. Instead, use this time to introduce yourself, explain how you are happy that he or she is in your class, and share something specific that the student has accomplished. Be aware of how you sound—be authentic and sincere in your praise.

- Send a congratulatory note home to the parent. This will be one note that the student will be sure to take home.

- Leave timely feedback on the student's work. Acknowledge when the student has made progress and be specific in your feedback. General comments like "Good Job and "Keep it up!" are not as effective as "Great job identifying the issue and supporting your argument."

- Give stickers. Yes, this even works for high school students. In doing so, recognize the specific act the student performed to earn the sticker.

- Spend a few minutes talking with the student. Let the student know that you appreciate how they are behaving.

- Acknowledge the student publicly.

You should also tell the students about the other rewards that come from following the classroom behavioral expectations, such as working in a safe and respectful environment, improved student learning, and improved grades. Communicate these positive outcomes both orally and in written form. Include them in a parent letter or create a daily visible reminder, such as a wall poster.

A clear and fair discipline policy benefits both teachers and students. The student teacher benefits by not being "put-on-the-spot" to come up with a punishment in response to bad behavior. This reduces your chances of becoming emotional and overreacting, ignoring the problem, or, worse, being perceived as inconsistent and unfair in applying your discipline policy. Your students will respect you more and your discipline issues will decrease. To achieve this, students must be acutely aware of the consequences for not meeting your expectations for classroom behavior.

You should develop a sequential series of consequences for repeat offences. Each step should be fair and appropriately matched to the behavior. For instance, do not administer a lunch detention for the first offence of talking out of turn. Rather, give the student a warning (preferably in a private manner) to stop talking. If the student continues then escalate to the next consequence, which may be a second warning, or lunch detention. Some common consequences include: warning, call or note home, time-out (reflection), lunch detention, school detention, or referral. Write down your sequence of consequences and clearly communicate it to your students. Finally, employ the Teaching Process (see Strategy 1) to evolve your discipline policy to meet the changing needs of the students.

I was not satisfied with my classroom discipline in the first few years of teaching. I felt that I wrote too many referrals. I brainstormed ways of tackling this issue through research, talking with colleagues, and reflection. I concluded that I needed a mechanism to keep minor offences from escalating into major problems. I built into my sequential consequences a reflection (time-out). For a minor discipline issue I would give one to two warnings. If the student's misbehavior continued, then I would give them the time-out for self-reflection. I would simply walk over to the student (being careful not disrupt the learning process) and discreetly hand him or her a paper to prompt reflection. The student was then to quietly go outside the classroom to complete the reflection. The reflection questions directly tied into the classroom behavior expectations. In the reflection, the student described the incident that led to this step, what expectation did they not meet, and how their actions affected their (and other's) learning. After a few minutes, I would join the student. I listened to their description and explanation of the incident. We discussed how it affected the class's expectations and learning. Before returning to class, I checked the student's understanding of the classroom expectations, and what the next consequence would be if their misbehavior continued. Meanwhile, I documented our conversation on the reverse side of the reflection paper, and later filed it.

The reflection paper proved to be a huge improvement in my discipline policy. In the two years following its implementation, I wrote only two referrals—a drastic decrease. The students benefited too, they felt that they were respected and their problems were "heard." Through this process, students save face, there is no power struggle, and the students are back in the learning environment within minutes.

As you create consequences for not meeting behavior expectations, it is critical to remember that you will have to follow through on them *consistently*. Wavering on your discipline policy will send confusing messages to your students. Enforce your discipline policy and you will earn genuine respect from the students. Too often, teachers lay out consequences to the students, but do not follow through. If the teacher told the students that they would get a lunch detention after a second warning, but does not give out lunch detentions, and just continues to give warning after warning, will the students then respect the teacher when it comes to discipline? The answer is a simple "absolutely not." Students would view this teacher as a softy and the teacher's discipline policy as ineffective.

During my second year of teaching, the school was reforming to improve student learning. As part of this reform process, staff collected data on the needs of the students, parents, and staff. We reviewed the results from the student surveys during a staff meeting. We were utterly shocked at the results. An overwhelming majority of the students surveyed ranked 'more discipline' in the classroom as their top need. Clearly, students do understand the need for structure and clear expectations in order for learning to take place. Students not only understand it, but they WANT IT!

Recommended Book

Discipline with Dignity

By Allen N. Mender and Richard L. Curwin

Association for Supervision and Curriculum Development, Alexandria, Virginia, 1999. P 35

Strategy 30

- - - - - - - - - - - -

Know Your Cooperating Teacher

I had a terrible education.
I attended a school for emotionally disturbed teachers.

— Woody Allen

In education, as in any field, we work with a range of people with different personalities and issues. Your choice of cooperating teaching may be completely out of your control. You may be partnered with a teacher that is supportive, or, on the other side of the spectrum, be paired with a teacher that is inflexible and unsupportive.

In my case, the cooperating teacher was supportive and provided me with an appropriate framework for teaching the class. She encouraged me to take pedagogical risks and try new ideas with the curriculum. She would assist me in any way possible and because of this, I owe a great deal to her. However, through my classroom observations and countless conversations with student teachers, I know that not every student teacher has a great cooperating teacher. The most common "bad" experience begins with a controlling cooperating teacher that demands, if not requires, that a certain curriculum be covered with a certain instructional delivery. Such cooperating teachers seem to be trying to create carbon copies of themselves, but only manage to stifle creativity. Alternatively, you may have a cooperating teacher that is not structured, more free flowing, and seems to create lesson plans while driving to work. This loose framework can cause problems because the student teacher is struggling to get their hands on something concrete (such as a curriculum) that they can work from. If either of these happen to you *do not despair*.

Approach the situation with a positive and forward-looking attitude. Continue to build a positive relationship with the cooperating teacher and regularly communicate some of the ideas you would like to try. If the cooperating teacher does not take to any of your ideas, solicit their advice on how to modify your idea in order for it to work in their classroom. Ninety-nine percent of the time this buy-in process will work, but if all else fails, remember that it is "easier to ask for forgiveness, than permission." But, do not do anything so drastic that it would jeopardize your relationship with the cooperating teacher or your student teaching grade. Keep in mind that you only have to work with this teacher for a short time, and soon it will be over. In a few months, you will have your own classroom where you can implement your pedagogical and curriculum ideas.

A Cooperating Teacher's Perspective

Advice for student teachers:

1. Consider the entire student teaching experience as an extended job interview: dress professionally, camouflage piercings and tattoos, and avoid sharing anecdotes of having been fired from a job or of substance-involved antics. Similarly, remember that it is acceptable to be friendly with students but not to be their friends. Resist the urge to share personal stories not related to curriculum, particularly if you teach at the secondary level. Come to work on time and don't cut out early. Be the ideal employee the school is looking to hire.

2. Listen more than you speak. It is typically the hallmark of the new teacher to go on and on about how they have been anointed as classroom deities and that they can hardly believe classrooms functioned before they set foot in one. It is great to think this; just keep it to yourself. If you listen to the experienced voices around you, you may pick up great tips.

3. Find amiable colleagues and eat lunch with them every day no matter how busy you are. It is healthy to be chummy with teachers other than just the one to which you are officially assigned.

4. Keep the main office (administration) happy. Turn in attendance and grades in a timely manner. Answer parent phone calls promptly.

5. Grade in the same manner as your cooperating teacher does. You can develop you own style later. Remember that your cooperating teacher will have to seamlessly take over again.

6. Visit other classrooms. Observe for alternate teaching and disciplinary styles as well as variances in organization (do they have bins, mailboxes, file folders, binders etc.?). Mentally file these observations for when you need to try something new.

7. It is O.K. to use the preservice experience to decide that teaching is not for you. Very few education candidates have any real insight into the actual day-to-day rigors of classroom teaching. For most of us, our only previous exposure is watching our own teachers, which fails to shed light on issues like strife between colleagues, tedium, administrative hassles, workload, hostile parents, and evaluation. Of course, it is also O.K. to discover what you love about teaching.

Leah Krippner, Cooperating Teacher

Strategy 31

Be Active With the School Community

The difference between involvement and commitment is like ham and eggs. The chicken is involved; the pig is committed.

— Martina Navratilova

A great strategy to differentiate yourself from other student teachers is through your level of involvement in the school community – outside the classroom. Think about how you can become an active member of the school community, what extracurricular activities you could participate in, which clubs, committees, or functions you could help with. List out some of your ideas and continue to add to them as you begin your student teaching.

There are real benefits to being involved in the school outside the classroom. Interactions with administration, staff, students, and parents outside the classroom are more relaxed and friendly, create more rapport, and leave a more lasting impression than on the few occasions you may have spoken to them inside the classroom. Moreover, when you engage in making the school a better place you demonstrate your commitment to the students and their education. In the process, you become a more appealing job candidate.

There is no doubt that your daily activities as a student teacher, such as setting up the classroom, teaching, preparing lesson plans, and grading will consume a large portion of your time. Inevitably, you will feel overwhelmed at times and, as a survival technique, it is important to find that line between mental breakdown and giving your all. One way to prevent utter exhaustion is to distinguish between being involved and making a commitment as a student teacher. An example of being involved means you assist in one or two sporting events in some capacity. An example of a commitment is that you promise to work at ALL of the games. Be wary when people ask you to do something on a continual basis; remember it is okay to take time to think about it and to say no. Rather, involve yourself in a few school community events that you feel are important instead of spreading yourself too thin through various commitments. This will prevent you from losing focus on your number one priority—student learning in the classroom.

Strategy 32

Think Customer Service

A satisfied customer is the best business strategy of all.

— Michael Leboeu

Another way to set yourself apart from other student teachers is to be more customer service focused. It is not surprising that my many years in customer service and business consulting affected how I approached teaching. I began by asking, who do I serve? What service do I offer? How can I best provide this service to the customer? I concluded that parents are my customers as they provide a significant portion of the funding for education (through private tuition or tax dollars or both). My service is to offer the best education to their children, along with excellent customer service.

How would you describe excellent customer service? What adjectives would you use? How could use incorporate this into your student teaching? Here are the top five traits that I believe defines excellent personal customer service:

- Competence

- Responsiveness

- Friendliness

- Listening

- Proactiveness

Competence

There is nothing more infuriating to a customer than dealing with an incompetent customer service representative. As a student teacher remember this and make every attempt to come across in every interaction with a parent as the professional, *competent* teacher that you are. If the parent (customer) challenges you on a certain decision, remain professional and support your decision with research or evidence. When you can reasonably support your decision, the parent will likely side with you or respectfully disagree.

Responsiveness

Secondly, try to be *responsive* to parents' inquiries: get into the habit of responding as soon as you can to their questions or concerns. Make a concerted effort to check your voicemail and email daily. If you need to do further research to answer a question, simply call or email the parent and let them know that you received their message, you are looking into it, and you will get back to them shortly. If you do not respond within a reasonable time, the parent will most likely take his or her question/concern to another teacher or the school administration. More importantly, understand that parents talk to each other. And if they feel they were ignored they will quickly let others know about it. This could negatively affect you as a student teacher.

Friendliness

Be *friendly* in every interaction with parents, even on those rotten days. Of course, try not to be overly friendly and come across as insincere. One trick I learned from customer service is that if you smile while you are talking on a phone, it will reflect in your voice and inflections.

Listening

How often have you called a helpline and the person on the other end does not seem to hear what you are saying? They simply are not *listening* to your concern, or they talk over you. It makes me want to scream, especially when the representative gives a scripted response that has nothing to do with my issue. As educators, *listening* is one of our most valuable tools. This is difficult sometimes because educators like to talk; it seems teachers always have an opinion. Sometimes, though, situations call for us to pause and listen, for example, to a parent concerned about a child's academic performance, or a grandmother concerned about a grandchild's possible gang involvement, or a student emotionally distraught because of peer bullying. Many times, your act of just listening allows the other party to release some pent-up frustrations. Once those frustrations have been aired, a true conversation can begin.

It was my second year of teaching, and it was parent teacher night. All the teachers assembled in the large common area, seated in rows just feet apart from each other. Parent after parent came and inquired about their child's performance. About halfway through the evening, a mother approached me about her son, who we will call Seth. Seth received a D on his report card for the 1st term, mainly because he performed poorly on a project, which included an individual and group component. Upon sitting, Seth's mother immediately asked why I gave Seth a D. I informed her it was due to his project grade. She told me that it was extremely unfair for me to grade Seth based on other's group member's efforts. I tried to explain that learning how to work in groups is vital, and she bit off my head.

"What? "You don't think I know what it takes in the real world? I am a school district employee, so do not pull any fast ones on me. It is unfair that others pulled my son's grade down. I want you to fix this right now."

I tried again to explain my grading and the rationale behind it and that I was not going to change his grade.

She responded, "You are incompetent. I am going to speak directly with the principal about you and your teaching practices." By this time, I was red-faced and was shaking with frustration and anger. My colleagues and other parents were witnessing this berating. Finally, I told her that there was nothing else I could do at that moment, since I did not have the project on hand. I informed her that I would review at her son's project to see how much the group grade pulled down Seth's grade after the conference.

Later that evening I went back to my classroom and found Seth's project. And to my surprise, Seth's group score was 83% and his individual score was 32%. It was the group component that pulled Seth's score up, and it was Seth that had pulled down the group grade a little. I quickly emailed off these findings to Seth's mother.

Driving home, I kept rerunning the incident in my head. How could have I handled that situation better? First, I should have let her air her concern, and then acknowledged it. Maybe I did not have to agree with it, but saying something like, "I understand what you are saying is that you don't think it's fair that Seth's grade should be pulled down because of others in the group. Is that correct?" Then follow-up by saying, "You have a valid concern. Even though the group grade represented 25% of his overall project grade, let me investigate how much the group affected his grade. Could I email or call you tomorrow about this?" I am almost certain that this approach would have prevented this parent from blowing up and making a scene. It would have only taken me a few minutes of active listening to resolve it.

Proactiveness

The final trait that characterizes fabulous customer service is being proactive—anticipating your customers' needs and responding to them. Being *proactive* is an important part of teaching, especially when dealing with parents. For instance, one of the top needs of parents is being informed of their child's social wellbeing and academic performance. You can satisfy this need by frequently emailing and calling parents, often through mass emails. When sending home parent letters, or during parent teacher conferences, solicit the parents' email addresses. Then you can send regular updates to the parents regarding your curriculum and upcoming school events. Once you have the email list it literally can take mere minutes to send an update. Another strategy is to call home or email when the student begins to show signs of poor performance – well before the students are in over their heads. Taking a proactive approach as a preservice teacher will differentiate you from your peers, and it provides you with concrete evidence of your communications with parents that may help in an interview.

Strategy 33

Socialize and Network Within Your School

**A successful social technique consists perhaps in finding
unobjectionable means for individual self-assertion.**

— Eric Hoffer

It is no secret that many preservice teachers get jobs at the school where
they were student teachers. This happens when a student teacher demonstrates
his or her skills and builds a trusting relationship with the staff. If the school in
which you are student teaching is a target school on your job search, then use
this opportunity to foster a positive relationship with your cooperating teacher
and the teachers you work closely with, such as team teachers or same
grade-level teachers.

Next, go beyond creating friendly relationships with teachers to include
other staff. Secretaries, janitors, food service workers, librarians, and computer
technicians all play vital roles in the school. Besides being great people, they can
be useful resources for your student teaching. You never know when your laptop
presentation will crash, or you need some emergency photocopies, or a second
helping of the day's mashed potatoes for additional energy. Moreover, they are
also working in the field of education. They may have friends and relatives in
other capacities and at other schools that may have useful job market insights.

Teachers are social by nature; if you meet up after work, then you certainly
should take advantage of this opportunity. Have fun, relax, and get to know
your colleagues on a more personal level. Be sure to keep an ear out for any
upcoming changes that could affect your hiring prospects. And if you can slip
it in, let the others know how much you enjoy teaching at that school, how you
appreciate the support the staff has shown, and how you would love to teach

there in the near future. Have control of the situation though. Do not drink too much or, worse yet, gossip about someone. You never know how this could come back to bite you.

Strategy 34

Build Your Touchstone

Desire is the key to motivation, but it's determination and commitment to an unrelenting pursuit of your goal – a commitment to excellence – that will enable you to attain the success you seek.

— Mario Andretti

Student teaching presents you with numerous opportunities to differentiate yourself from the other thousands of student teachers. One way to do so is by establishing a touchstone early in your student teaching. A touchstone is a standard by which something is judged. You want to establish a standard of excellence (a touchstone) that improves targeted student learning, through instruction or a curriculum, and that is easily transferable to another school.

With today's high-stakes testing, principals are seeking out job candidates that can analyze students' test results to identify areas of improvement in reading, writing, math, and possibly science. Principals also want to know how you have improved student learning in those targeted areas, and how you could impact student learning in their schools.

Identify Areas of Improvement

Certainly, every teacher plays a part in improving the students' skills in reading, writing, and math, regardless of what particular subjects or areas you are certified in. But, you need to strike a balance between teaching these skill sets and teaching your curriculum. In establishing your touchstone, you should begin by focusing most of your effort in improving one particular area. Use student data, such as student work, or school-wide standardized testing, to determine what this focus area should be.

Establish a Baseline

Let us imagine that you have scrutinized your school's recent standardized test scores. You notice that in the areas of writing and math, the students' scores have progressed significantly from last year. However, the reading scores showed only slight improvement and continue to lag behind the district and state average scores. From this data, you resolve to incorporate reading skills in your curriculum in hopes of increasing students' reading comprehension, and, ultimately, the students' test results.

The next step is to establish a baseline for your area of improvement, which in this example is reading comprehension in your classroom. This will enable you to 1) determine the skill level in your particular classroom, and 2) create a standard through which you can measure progress. Here are some ways to determine a baseline on the students' learning and skill level:

- Surveys

- Sample project work

- Quizzes

- Teacher observations

- Standardized tests

- Student reflections

Example

Let us say that you have quizzed your students after they read an article. You also gave them a survey that asked the students to identify the different reading strategies they employed while reading the article. Your survey lists various best-practice reading strategies with descriptive examples and the students mark the ones they used. From the collected surveys, you build your baseline by formulating some quantitative findings. For instance, you determine that only 15% of your students use two or more of the best-practice reading strategies. In addition, 65% of the students indicated they had "difficulty" in comprehending the article. Next, you grade the quizzes and find a class average score of 62%. The survey findings shed some light as to why the students scored poorly on the reading comprehension quiz. You realize that the students use very few reading strategies to improve their comprehension, and this is reflected in their assessments. The good news is you now have a clearer view of the problem and you have a measurable baseline (the quantitative analysis) to determine if using reading strategies will improve the students' reading comprehension.

Build your Touchstone

To form your touchstone you must become a reflective problem solver. Begin by brainstorming ways of tackling the problem of improving your students' baseline. You may want to incorporate best practices you learned in your teacher education training. Another great tool for figuring out how to implement effective strategies is collaboration with other teachers. For instance, if improving reading comprehension were my focus then I would partner up with the Language Arts teachers to investigate effective reading strategies. There are other means to generate your plan of action:

- Reading literature

- Researching educational journals

- Observing classrooms in which students are exhibiting proficiency in your area of improvement

- Partnering with your local university

- Attending professional development workshops

- Searching the Internet

Once you have determined the best practice instructional strategies and/or changes to make in your curriculum, the next step is implementation. You begin to teach the students how to monitor their reading comprehension, employ "fix-it" strategies when the students' comprehension falls off, and introduce tools discovered during your research, such as double entry journals.

Soon after implementation, evaluate your plan of action to see if what you are doing is influencing the bottom-line: your students' learning. Using the same assessment tools (in this example, a survey and quiz) you develop a quantitative analysis. Compared to the baseline, have the students shown any significant improvement in your targeted area of improvement, i.e., reading comprehension?

Lastly, reflect on and tweak your plan of action to get even greater results. Do not limit your thinking to improving learning in just that classroom, but think about how you could use these strategies in another school with a similar learning need.

If you are able to accomplish this feat during your already hectic student teaching time, then consider yourself are a teaching rock star. And you now have a concrete example of student improvement to discuss at future job interviews. In such discussions, articulate all the steps you took: from collecting and analyzing the data, setting student-learning goals, researching the methodology, implementing your plan, to evaluating and reflecting on the results. Describe how this process impacted student learning by providing concrete figures, such as student comprehension improved by 23% over six months. Finally, show how the standards you set at the school where you were a student teacher could be applicable to other schools. For instance, "Reviewing the state tests, I (the job candidate) noticed the students' reading scores at your (principal's) school are similar to the school where I was a student teacher. I strongly believe I would be able to deliver the same improvements in reading comprehension to ABC High School as I did in XYZ High School." Having a touchstone of excellence will greatly enhance your chances of being hired in the school you desire.

Strategy 35

Organize Your Teaching Portfolio

I wish I knew what was next. I got this movie without planning to. I'm really excited to be continuing in film because it's a great job but I have my portfolio and resume for any other opportunity.

– Colleen Haskell

As a student teacher, you will need to build on the teaching portfolio you constructed in your teacher education program (see Strategy 6). Although you do not absolutely need a portfolio to land a teaching job, it is advisable to have one ready for interviews. The truth is, you will be lucky if a principal spends more than a few minutes perusing your portfolio. Therefore, your portfolio should be well-organized and focused on three important areas from your student teaching experience that tell a principal about you and your work:

- Professional growth
- Sample work (student work, projects, rubrics, etc.)
- Standards

Professional Growth

This section usually consists of a series of typed reflections (three is usually enough) on such topics as your professional goals, instructional strategies, and assessments of student learning.

Begin by reflecting on your student goals. Did you meet them? How did you meet them? How do you know? If you did fail to meet your student teaching goals, explain why. Next, reflect on the various instructional strategies and assessments you used. Which instructional strategies worked best? How did you assess the students' learning? Provide examples throughout your reflections. What have you learned that you would apply at your next teaching position? You could also write further reflections on classroom management, your touchstone, and your curriculum.

Finally, if you received favorable classroom observations and evaluations from your clinical supervisor and/or your cooperating teacher then include those in your professional growth section. Principals do like to see how others evaluated your teaching.

Sample Work

"The proof is in the pudding." Principals will want to see how well your students have performed under your tutelage, and will evaluate you based on your students' work. Reviewing your rubrics, projects, and student artifacts will give principals an insight into your teaching that they cannot get by simply reading your philosophy statements.

Here are a few simple steps to get started on this section of your portfolio:

1) Choose 1-2 units, lessons, or projects completed by your students. You may also want to highlight your touchstone (see Strategy 34).

2) Include project descriptions, your instructions to the students, lesson plans, and rubrics in a sequential and meaningful order.

3) Enclose student work that is both stellar and not so stellar. Be sure to include specific and productive feedback on all the students' work. Principals will want to see how you grade and provide feedback (see Strategy 24).

4) Include sample work for special education and ELL students.

5) Protect your students' privacy by erasing or blackening out any personal information.

Standards

Standards and grade level expectations are critical elements in education. Your portfolio is an excellent opportunity to demonstrate your awareness of education standards and provide examples of how you met those standards in your classroom. List out several standards and provide a description of how you met them.

Other Suggestions

- Scan your portfolio's contents, especially student work, into PDF format and create CDs to distribute during the interview.

- Upload your portfolio to the Internet. Be careful not to divulge any personal information, which could open the door to identity theft (see Strategy 6).

- Carefully proofread your portfolio.

- Ask your clinical supervisor and cooperating teacher to review your portfolio.

Strategy 36

Thank Your Network

**My first job is to say thank you to those who voted for me.
Those who didn't, I'm going to get your vote next time.**

— Barack Obama

In the flurry of wrapping up your final days of student teaching, do not forget
to thank the individuals who provided you with support. Review your network
list (see Strategy 15) and make a note of all those you need to thank. A 'thank
you' can be a card, a simple note, or a gift—for those who went that extra mile.
I recommend sending a short thank you note to anybody that helped you. For
your cooperating teacher, team teachers, and clinical supervisor, who provide
guidance and support throughout your student teaching experience, a thoughtful
gift with a card is appropriate. Take some time to think about your interactions
with these individuals and let them know how they have affected you and your
teaching practices.

Let us not forget the students. A nice send off and thank you to the students
would mean a lot to them.

One of my colleagues wrote an individualized thank you note to
each of her students. She was an elementary school teacher so
she spent most of her workday with her 20 students and had
developed deep relationships with them. On the other hand, I
had over 100 students, so I just spent a few minutes thanking
the classes for their support and telling them what the experience
meant for me. At the end of class, I stood and shook each
student's hand as they left.

Some others we should not forget are your family and friends that put up with your rants and stress over the past several months. They are often the bedrock of our lives and need to be reminded how important they are to us.

Find Your Ideal Teacher Job

Strategy 37

Shine After Student Teaching

It takes a long time to educate a community and it can't be done by spellbinders, moneybags, hypnotizers, magicians, or Aladdin's lamp. Character is what matters on a paper.

— Harry J. Grant

Well done—you have completed your student teaching training. As your student days wind down you may have a few months of relative calm before the hiring season begins (usually in June and going through August). During this period, you can increase your chance of being hired by networking and diversifying your skill sets.

Take Additional Coursework

Enrolling in additional courses will broaden your skills and knowledge. Consider pursuing additional endorsements or certification in high-need areas such as ELL (English Language Learners) or Special Education. Even if you do not earn an endorsement or certification, there are numerous benefits to taking additional courses. For one, you will know more about how to meet your students' learning needs. You will also have a strong foundation should you decide, in the future, to pursue extra certification. Extra courses will also make you more appealing to principals and hiring committees.

Substitute Teach or Coach

"No more coursework!" you may be thinking. This is completely understandable. The good news is there are many other ways to expand your value as a job candidate. Substitute teaching and coaching are excellent ways to strengthen your teaching skills and get the proverbial "foot in the door." While substitute teaching and coaching, continue to expand your network. Keep records on the teachers and schools you substituted for–organizational tools such as your network spreadsheet will make this a breeze (see Strategy 15). Also, while teaching or coaching, remember to try to become a familiar face in the school (see Strategy 14).

Volunteer

If you cannot find a substitute teaching or coaching position, then consider becoming active in your local community. Teachers are known for their commitment to their community. Many teachers and administrators volunteer great amounts of their time for causes that are important to them. Find a cause that you are passionate about, such as homelessness, hunger, the environment, and local school improvement. Start by calling your local city government, or visiting their website, to get a list of volunteer opportunities that might interest you, such as the Boy/Girl Scouts, Rotary Clubs, Kiwanis, YMCA, Red Cross, and United Way. You may find yourself rubbing shoulders with people in positions to help you obtain that desired teacher job. In addition to helping the community, you are building and using your skills, networking with others, and polishing your resume to reflect your civic-minded activities.

Strategy 38

Craft an Effective Resume

The resume explains your experience, what kinds of classes you taught, your school improvement, and any co-curricular activities you directed. The resume will help make the final sale to secure a place on the interview list.

— Robert W. Pollock, Ed.D.

There is a vast amount of information available on resume writing in hundreds of books, countless magazine articles, and numerous career workshops devoted to this topic alone. This one section can only supplement a more thorough examination of resume writing. When I worked in business, I reviewed many thousands of resumes. In doing so, I identified some essential elements needed for every resume, and put together some tips on how to make your resume more effective.

Your resume has two important functions. First, it highlights your achievements (professional and academic) and community involvement. Secondly, your resume shows prospective employers that you are qualified for the job for which you are applying by showing how your skills meet the job specifications. It should come as no surprise, then, that since you have a diverse background and the jobs you are applying for vary in duties and responsibilities you will need more than one version of your resume.

Every resume has the same components—contact information, education, and experience. Your resume may also have:

- Objective
- Certification Information
- Community Involvement
- Special skills

Resume Components

Personal Contact Information

This section is self-explanatory; it should include your name, address, phone number, email address, and any other information that you think would assist a principal or hiring committee in contacting you. Please note that if you are working from an older resume template you should check that your information is correct. Silly as it may seem I have had numerous incidents where I went to call a qualified candidate for an interview and the phone number on the resume was incorrect.

JOHN C. DOE

1234 8th Avenue	Tel: (312) 555-1234
Chicago, IL 60120	johna1234@hotmail.com

Objective

It is not essential to include a career objective in your resume. More and more experts are saying that an objective is a waste of scarce space that could be used to highlight another skill or accomplishment. On the other hand, some hiring managers prefer resumes with an objective because it allows them to easily sort and file resumes according to job openings. If you include one, your objective statement should be concise and specific to the job for which you are applying. The sample statement (below) is right to the point and lets the hiring manager know what the job seeker wants.

Objective

Enthusiastic educator seeking a Social Studies teacher position in the Chicago Public Schools

---

Education and Certification

Include here the degrees you have received, name(s) of the school(s) you graduated from, dates of graduation, and any other studies that contribute to your qualifications as a teacher. If you do not have a lot of work experience, then highlight your academic successes, such as awards or honors you have received. Only include your GPA if it is 3.0 or higher.

Education and Certification

Master of Arts in Teaching
Loyola University

Chicago, IL
May 2004

Bachelor of Arts in Education
DePaul University

Chicago, IL
May 2001

Illinois Teaching Certificate
Endorsements in Social Studies and ELL

Effective 2004 - 2008

Experience

In many resumes, this section is often too cumbersome and wordy. Some misguided job seekers believe their chances are diminished if they have not listed all their skills and experiences. On the contrary, the purpose of your resume is to highlight your most important skills and experiences and show how they relate to the job for which you are applying. You can discuss your skills and experience in more depth in your interview.

Hiring principals have limited time, and may skip over long-winded explanations of work history. In writing your resume, prioritize your most important skills and experiences; then highlight them with bullets. Be concise and clear in your writing using action words to begin each skill and experience.

Teaching Experience

ABC High School
Business Education Teacher

Seattle, WA
September 2006 - Present

- Teaches Introduction to Information Technology and Business Law
- Advises school's business club, Future Business Leaders of America
- Instituted and advises Seattle's only Competitive Mock Trial Team
- Developed and team-taught an integrated, project-based curriculum that engages students' higher-level thinking through service learning
- Created a fun and innovative math preparation program for freshmen advisories
- Won Seattle Rotary's Teacher of the Month (October 2007)

On the next page there is a table of sample teacher specific action words to assist in your resume writing.

Table 38.1

Action Words for Teacher Resume

Abstracted	Conceived	Instituted	Provided
Achieved	Conducted	Integrated	Publicized
Acquired	Conserved	Investigated	Published
Acted	Consulted	Judged	Received
Adapted	Contracted	Kept	Reduced
Addressed	Contributed	Launched	Referred
Administered	Counseled	Learned	Related
Advertised	Created	Mentored	Relied
Advised	Critiqued	Met	Reported
Advocated	Cultivated	Minimized	Researched
Applied	Dealt	Modeled	Responded
Appraised	Designed	Modified	Restored
Approved	Detected	Monitored	Revamped
Arranged	Determined	Narrated	Set goals
Ascertained	Developed	Negotiated	Shaped
Augmented	Devised	Observed	Skilled
Authored	Established	Obtained	Strategized
Bolstered	Estimated	Offered	Solved
Briefed	Evaluated	Operated	Strengthened
Brought	Examined	Ordered	Stressed
Budgeted	Exceeded	Organized	Studied
Built	Excelled	Originated	Substantiated
Calculated	Expanded	Practiced	Succeeded
Cared	Expedited	Predicted	Summarized
Chaired	Experimented	Prepared	Synthesized
Collaborated	Explained	Presented	Supervised
Collected	Explored	Prioritized	Supported
Comforted	Expressed	Produced	Surveyed
Communicated	Extracted	Programmed	Sustained
Compared	Facilitated	Projected	Symbolized
Completed	Fashioned	Promoted	Tabulated
Complied	Influenced	Proposed	Talked
Composed	Initiated	Protected	Taught
Computed	Inspected	Proved	Visualized

Other Advice

Your resume should be a reflection of you. All of the work that goes into preparing a resume is important, from what information to include (and leave out) to the style and layout. Get outside opinions on how to improve the look of your resume by asking colleagues, family, and friends (see Strategy 39).

During your job search, you will most likely create several drafts of your resume and will need different versions to meet all the needs of your job search. Try to think of your resume as a living document that you will need to regularly review and update. Do not to destroy or delete your old resumes. You never know when you may have to search back through them to pull out employment history or skills that you omitted on your latest version and now need to include.

Finally, before you send your resume to prospective employers, I suggest proofreading it at least five times. One item to look for is whether you used any personal pronouns, like "I." A professional resume will never have "I" in it, so be sure to reword your sentence. Check carefully for spelling and grammatical errors, as many employers, myself included, will just toss out any resume with such errors.

A Principal's Perspective

Here is an important reminder from a principal:

As for the resume, please have it fit to one page. Remember the resume should include your highlights. You will have the chance to give examples of your achievements in the interview.

Kathryn Hutchinson, High School Principal

Strategy 39

Ask (The Right Person) For Help on Your Resume

Anything that's worth having is worth asking for.
Some say yes and some say no.

— **Melba Colgrove**

A gutsy, but creative strategy is to review your resume with a principal—perhaps at the school where you were a student teacher. Politely ask your principal to set up a time to review your resume. When you do this, you should be ready to hand over a hard copy or email an electronic version of your documents. Let the principal know that you would appreciate his or her valuable insight on how to improve the effectiveness of your resume and cover letter.

There are some real benefits to having face time with a school principal about your resume. For one, the conversation is really about you and your qualifications and may just be the catalyst that shifts a principal's view of you from "preservice teacher" to a "highly-qualified job candidate." Once the principal has made that shift, and you have had a chance to share some your experiences in an informal setting, the principal may divulge job leads to you, or might even go as far as putting in good word for you at a hiring school.

The obvious benefit of arranging this meeting is to receive feedback from the type of person that will be hiring you. Bring an extra draft of your documents for you to make notes on as you review them. In the course of your conversation, solicit specific suggestions to polish up your resume. Ask the principal if there are any important accomplishments you may have omitted on your resume. Again, this allows the principal to focus on you and your skill sets.

If for some reason you are not able to arrange a meeting with the principal then connect with others in your school network: teacher colleagues, librarians, cooperating teacher, professors, and clinical supervisor. You could also send out your resume to family and friends for their feedback, and ask them to look for any spelling, grammatical, and formatting errors.

Strategy 40

--- -- -- -- -- -- -- -- --

Establish a Credential File

**A credential file is a packet of background information that is
sent to a prospective employer when a candidate is applying for
a professional position. Files are most frequently established for
elementary and secondary school teachers, school administrators,
college and university professors, school counselors, speech
pathologists and other school specialty areas.**

—University of Central Missouri Career Services

In many ways, applying for a teaching position is similar to applying to college,
especially in the list of things you need to send to a prospective employer, such
as an application, resume or CV, official college transcripts, recommendation
letters, and written essays. Like college applications, a job search is time
consuming. It takes a lot of effort to research job openings, compile your
application package, and track your work. A little organization can go a long way
towards reducing the stress associated with your job search. One great strategy
for organizing and streamlining your job search is establishing a credential file.
A credential file, also known as a placement file, is a file containing all your
important documents that can be sent to potential employers.

The very first step in setting up your credential file is gathering all your
necessary documents: resume, recommendation letters, references, official
transcripts, sample work, and evaluations. Begin this step as early as you can—
preferably early April. It may take weeks to obtain your transcripts and to get
recommendation letters from college professors, clinical supervisors, principals,
and teachers.

Once you have your documents in place, ask your school's career service office if they offer a credential file service. After you place all your papers into your credential file with your school's career service office, you will be able to ask them to send it to prospective employers. Career service offices will charge a fee for creating the credential file and for a set number of copies to be sent. For instance, a career service office may charge $25–30 to send out 10 copies of your credential file to prospective employers. If your school's career services office does not offer a credential file service then consider establishing an electronic credential file with a reputable online company, such as Interfolio (www.interfolio.com). These companies allow you to submit your documents by uploading them to their website, or by mailing them to their processing centers. They will then send your files to prospective employers identified by you.

There are many advantages to this system of credential files. For one, you save a lot of time by not having to print out and copy all those documents every time you apply for a job. Instead, you simply fill out a paper or electronic request indicating where you want specific documents to be sent. Secondly, maintaining a credential file at your school may save you money in the long run. Many hiring school districts require official transcripts, but they will often accept copied official transcripts sent directly from your school's career services office, or a reputable online service. This saves you the money you would otherwise have to spend on the fees for requesting official transcripts from your undergraduate and graduate schools.

But, there are several issues to consider with such services. Most importantly, carefully review all the fees charged for the service, from the setup fees to the cost of mailing out your credential file. Find out how long the turnaround time is between when you submit your request and when your credential file will be mailed. Be sure to keep an updated resume on file. You do not want to mail outdated resumes to prospective employers. Finally, keep at least one backup copy of your credential file with you in case of an emergency.

Strategy 41

- - - - - - - - - - - -

Double-check Your Certification

A man should not leave this earth with unfinished business.
He should live each day as if it was a pre-flight check.
He should ask each morning, am I prepared to lift-off?

— Diane Frolov & Andrew Schneider,
Northern Exposure, *All is Vanity*, 1991

Are you prepared to take off and land your dream job? One of the most critical items for you to have is your certification. Any delay in obtaining your appropriate certification will inevitably result in a delay in getting a teaching job. Start by visiting the website for your state's education office responsible for teacher certification. Double-check your state's certification process timeframe to see how long it will take to obtain your credentials. Next, determine if you have all the required paperwork – signatures, fingerprints, and supporting papers – in place to avoid any delays. Be sure to make copies of your complete certification application before you submit it. If you have not received notification or certification within the timeframe described on the website, call the state education office immediately to ask about your certification.

Strategy 42

Be Aware of the Hiring Timeframe

**Frustration, although quite painful at times,
is a very positive and essential part of success.**

— Bo Bennett

Inevitably, the one question on almost every future teacher's mind is, "When do I begin looking for a teaching job?" To answer this, you should evaluate what type of teaching position you want. Begin by asking yourself these four questions:

1) What subjects would you prefer to teach?

2) What grade levels would you prefer?

3) What school(s) do you want to apply to?

4) What are the geographical boundaries of your job search?

In answering these questions, you will create a clearer vision of your ideal job. Take care not to narrow your focus too much and overlook other job opportunities. The key is to maintain a balance between searching for what you really want and not severely limiting your job opportunities.

Armed with your vetted resume, cover letter, and credential file, immediately start your job search by researching on the Internet, pouring over your local newspaper want ads, attending career fairs, reading district job postings, speaking to your school's career office, and utilizing your most powerful weapon—your network.

Below is an assessment of the hiring conditions for each month leading up to the next school year. This monthly assessment will also provide concrete actions a soon-to-be teacher can take to improve the likelihood of being hired.

April

April is a good month to start browsing job listings to find out what positions are available. Carefully check to see if any open positions are for the next school year or for the current year only. While browsing the job openings, keep a note of which positions are in high demand and in what schools. Read carefully the job descriptions that accompany the job openings to find out the job certification requirements and what employers are looking for in a job candidate. But, be aware that some school districts will not consider applications for the next school year until after a certain date, and April may be too early.

May and June

May and June are the busiest months for hiring teachers. Principals want the first shot at attracting and hiring the best teachers from the available teacher-candidate pool. Many principals say that if they what until July or August to hire, the applicant pool will be smaller and it is more difficult to find a highly qualified teacher. In addition, as the school year ends, teachers announce retirements, transfers, or resignations, so principals will want move quickly to fill these vacancies.

July

Hiring activity slows in July. Many principals plan their vacations during this time, resulting in fewer opportunities for you to secure an interview. But, do not become discouraged and completely dismiss July. Interviews and hiring still take place in July.

August and early September

Hiring picks back up in August and September as principals try to fill remaining vacancies, as well as last minute teacher transfers and retirements. For teachers still searching for a job, anxiety and frustration builds in these months. Use this to your advantage by doubling your efforts to find a job. Begin by looking for ways to broaden your search. Ask yourself these questions: Are you endorsed in other areas? Are you willing to widen your geographical area to include other school districts? Are there alternative teaching positions that you could take in the interim?

Preservice teachers often ask, "When should I begin to worry about not having a job?" From my own experience, and from speaking with numerous principals, the time to really worry is about one to two weeks before school starts. If you do find yourself in this spot (as I did), do not despair. It is crucial that you try to be as positive and optimistic as you can. It comes down to this: schools are in need of great teachers such as yourself, so you will find a job.

Strategy 43

- - - - - - - - - - - -

Track Your Job Search

Don't agonize. Organize.

— Florynce Kennedy

You will probably be applying for numerous teaching positions, in many different schools, and in many school districts. You will also be involved in a flurry of job-related activities, including researching new job positions, writing an essay for a job posting, requesting your credential file be mailed to a hiring school, and calling a principal to follow up on a submitted application.

You will need a useful tool to help you organize and keep track of all these activities. A spreadsheet program such as Microsoft Excel™ is a good option. Alternatively, you can establish a free Google™ account (www.google.com) that will give you access to their service called Docs and Spreadsheets. The Google™ spreadsheet is web-based, but it has the same basic functionality of Excel™.

Format your spreadsheet to track job positions you are interested in. Include columns for updates on a job's status and to note persons you have spoken and when you spoke to them. Add a to-do-list. See Table 43.1 for an example.

Using a spreadsheet that tracks your contacts allows for better follow-up and reduces unnecessary and potentially harmful errors, such as forgetting who you spoke to on the phone about an interview. Make a habit of updating your contact tracking spreadsheet regularly and especially after every important step in your job search. These simple actions will help manage the chaos that comes with a job search.

Table 43.1

Last Updated	School District	School	Position of Interest	Contact Name and Info	Status	To Do
5/5	ABC District	ABC High School	Business Education FTE 1.0	Joe Smith Principal (555)555-5555	5/3 – Found posting 5/4 – Requested credential file 5/5 – Sent in app. & materials	5/10 – Place call with principal to set up interview

Strategy 44

Draw From Your Network

When shooting in the dark, it is a good idea to use a machine gun.

— Craig Bruce

If you have developed and organized a network of friends and colleagues, then this is the time to use it (see Strategies 13–17, 33, and 36 for advice on how to build a network). Do not shy away from sending monthly or quarterly updates on your life, and, more specifically, on the status of your job search to your network. Ask your friends and colleagues to contact you if they hear of any teacher job openings or soon-to-be openings. A simple email here and there will suffice as friendly reminders to your network to keep an eye out for your interests.

Your network also serves functions other than finding you your dream teaching job. More than likely your network includes people with whom you have an authentic and meaningful relationship. Rely on those people for support and advice. A meeting with a colleague at a local coffee shop may serve as a refreshing reminder that your job hunting struggles are not happening in isolation. Phoning an old friend may lead to a wonderful volunteer opportunity. From your university professors to your cooperating teachers it is now time to utilize your network; you never know what doors of opportunity may be opened. Remember—you can track these interactions as described in Strategy 15 and 43.

Strategy 45

Practice Interview Questions

**The passion to teach is already inside your heart,
but you need to secure a position you truly want and
work in the district that best meets your needs.
To reach that goal, you need to prepare for the
interviews you will receive.**

— Robert W. Pollock, Ed.D.

You can set yourself up for a successful interview by being properly prepared, which will in turn boost your self-confidence and increase your chances of being hired.

While self-confidence plays an important role in giving an effective interview, a lack of preparation can easily destroy any chances of success. A prepared job candidate will never be totally surprised by a question in an interview. Certainly, there will be an unexpected question or two, but the effective candidate will always be able to respond to interview questions in a thoughtful and deliberate manner.

To start, take some time to reflect on your experiences and the training that has brought you to this point. Read your reflective notes (see Strategies 1 and 3), consider the coursework and books that inspired you (see Strategies 2 and 4), and think back on your student teaching experiences (see Strategies 22-34). This exercise will help you realize that you are fully prepared and worthy to start your journey as a teacher.

The next step in your preparation is researching questions frequently asked in interviews for teaching positions. From consultations with numerous principals, and by gathering questions that my colleagues and I were asked – in one form or another – during our interviews, I have compiled a list of several important interview questions. Take a moment and write down your thoughts on how you might respond to these questions:

- What is your approach to / philosophy on teaching?
- Describe a motivating teacher.
- Suggest some reasons why students misbehave.
- What is your approach to classroom management?
- Describe your idea of an extraordinary teacher.
- What will make you an excellent teacher in 5 years, or 10 years?
- Describe how you plan your lessons.
- Why should you be hired over other job applicants?

In an interview be sure to answer the questions you were asked; stay "on message" and be concise. You can avoid rambling answers by responding with no more than three key points per question. Briefly elaborate on each key point; better yet, provide an example from your school, work, and/or volunteer experience. If the interviewers need more information they will ask for further clarification.

Practice Interview Questions

What is your approach to or philosophy on teaching?

Interviewers ask this question is to find out your guiding principles for education. Prepare for interviews by re-reading your education philosophy statement (see Strategy 18). Outline your top three core beliefs on teaching and student learning and describe specific examples of how your philosophy has informed your curriculum and instruction methods.

Sample answer

I believe in instilling a passion for lifetime learning into my students. One way I instill this passion is by being a model lifetime learner for my students. For instance, in my classroom, you will hear me thinking aloud, interacting with the text during reading, and demonstrating inquiry by asking questions.

I believe that every child can reach their learning potential, with high expectations, the necessary support and opportunities, and a caring classroom. I support this effort by greeting each child as he/she enters the classroom, so that each student feels welcome and believes that he/she is part of a learning community. I clearly state the learning and behavioral expectations for my class, and I follow through in upholding these standards. For instance, if a student turns in a substandard project, then I meet with the student, reiterate my expectations, and provide any further assistance or support that the student might need to finish the project.

I believe in teaching students with dignity, and in providing a fun, student-centered learning environment. I make sure that every child knows that is they are worthy, by listening to and caring for their needs. I work hard to create a classroom that celebrates achievement and progress. These efforts encourage the students to stay in school and learn. Weekly celebrations in the form of specific task praise, certificates, positive calls home, and group recognition are common in my classroom. By the end of the school year, each child will be celebrated for some contribution to the class or a skill they have developed.

Describe a motivating teacher

Another way of phrasing this question is, "How will you create a classroom environment through which you will motivate your students." You can take a number of approaches to answer this common interview question, such as: classroom management, learning environment, instruction, teacher and student relationship, and curriculum. One successful approach to answering this question is to address an overarching theme, such as *establishing clear and high expectations for your students.* Students will be motivated to learn and behave properly when they internalize the teacher's expectations. For instance, if a student walked into your classroom on any given day

- Can the student expect a certain daily routine?

- Can the students expect to be treated fairly when discipline is used?

- Will the student know the overarching learning objective or essential question for a lesson?

All of these provide an environment that encourages students to learn from you. In answering these questions try to create a visual picture for the interviewers of your classroom. In your depiction, explain how you set clear and high expectations from the start of class to the dismissal bell.

What is your approach to classroom management?

Classroom management is important and has many implications for the school administration. First, if you – as a classroom teacher – can create effective classroom management then you have cleared a path to higher and sustained learning. It is nearly impossible to create a learning environment in a classroom that is disrespectful, disorderly, and dysfunctional. Boundaries on behavior and expectations for learning need to be clear to students and consistently enforced (see Strategy 29). Effective classroom management also translates into less work for the school administration. The teacher that routinely sends students down to the principal and writes a fistful of disciplinary referrals increases workloads and headaches for administrators. Not to mention those "problem" students on their way to the principal's office are missing out on learning opportunities in the classroom.

Therefore, it is critical that you have a strong response to this question. If you cannot articulate your classroom management plan, then how can you expect to manage a classroom full of students?

In answering this question, think of your broad classroom management philosophy (see Strategies 27 and 28). Follow this up with a personal triumph involving classroom management and then relate this example to your philosophy. For instance, in one interview I explained my belief that relationships, routines, and rigor are critical components of effective classroom management and provided concrete examples of how I incorporate them in daily class work.

Describe an extraordinary teacher

This is a very personal interview question, as it touches on your beliefs and education philosophy. Consider how an outstanding teacher touched your life. How did that teacher positively affect your life? What qualities or traits did this teacher have that you would want to emulate as a beginning teacher (e.g., created engaging lessons, infused humor into the classroom)? How did that teacher manage their classroom? How did that teacher build trusting and respectful relationships with the students? Did this teacher believe in you more than you believed in yourself? By answering these questions, you will develop a meaningful answer to this question.

What will make you a great teacher in 5 or 10 years?

Understanding personal and professional growth is essential to evolving into a master teacher. Research shows that pursuit of professional development, disciplined self-reflection, and establishing collaborative time with colleagues are characteristics of an effective teacher. Describe how you have embraced these best practices and the impact it has had on your students' learning.

Describe how you plan your lessons

In asking this question, hiring principals are trying to find out how you approach certain elements during your lesson planning, including learning objectives, standards, assessments, activities, special accommodations, and reflection.

Effective lesson planning begins with establishing desired learning outcomes or goals for the students. These learning outcomes should be based on "higher order thinking." Familiarize yourself Dr. Bloom's work on the categories of student thinking, from the lower order thinking skills (knowledge, comprehension, and application) to the higher order thinking skills (analysis, synthesis, and evaluation). Thoroughly review the Bloom's example below. The example includes verb outcomes, coupled with categories of thinking (Krumme, 2005). This information will assist you in your lesson planning and in answering this interview question.

Bloom's Lower Order Thinking

1. Knowledge is remembering appropriate, previously learned information. This level of thinking is illustrated by students defining, describing, enumerating, identifying, labeling, listing, matching, naming, reading, recording, reproducing, selecting, stating, and/or viewing.

2. Comprehension is the understanding of the meaning of informational materials. This level of thinking is illustrated by students classifying, citing, converting, describing, discussing, estimating, explaining, generalizing, giving examples, making sense out of, paraphrasing, summarizing, tracing, and/or understanding.

3. Application is the use of previously learned information in new and concrete situations to solve problems that have single or best answers. This level of thinking is illustrated by students *acting, administering, articulating, assessing, charting, collecting, computing, constructing, contributing, controlling, determining, developing, discovering, establishing, extending, implementing, including, informing, instructing, participating, predicting, preparing, preserving, producing, projecting, providing, relating, reporting, showing, solving, teaching, transferring, using, and/or utilizing.*

Bloom's Higher Order Thinking

4. Analysis is the breaking down of information into its component parts, examining the information to develop conclusions, making inferences, and/or finding evidence to support generalizations. This level of thinking is illustrated by students *correlating, diagramming, differentiating, discriminating, distinguishing, focusing, illustrating, inferring, limiting, outlining, pointing out, prioritizing, recognizing, separating, and/or subdividing.*

5. Synthesis is creating a new product using prior knowledge and skills. This level of thinking is illustrated by students *adapting, anticipating, categorizing, collaborating, combining, communicating, comparing, compiling, composing, contrasting, creating, designing, devising, expressing, facilitating, formulating, generating, incorporating, individualizing, initiating, integrating, intervening, modeling, modifying, negotiating, planning, progressing, rearranging, reconstructing, reinforcing, reorganizing, revising, structuring, substituting, and/or validating.*

6. Evaluation is determining value and providing a rationale for the response. This level of thinking is illustrated by students *appraising, comparing and contrasting, concluding, criticizing, critiquing, deciding, defending, interpreting, judging, justifying, reframing, and/or supporting.*

Next in your lesson planning process, describe how these learning outcomes connect to the curriculum benchmarks, and district and state standards. After that, stress the importance of assessment in determining if the students have met the stated learning outcomes. Use the outcome-illustrating verbs (above), from Bloom's Taxonomy, to evaluate the students' learning. Your response should also show how effective teachers use a wide variety of assessment techniques, and use those assessments to give valuable feedback to their students and to encourage their improvement. Assessment is much more than paper tests and final "no more chances" tests.

Once you have shown how you establish learning objectives and assessments, hiring principals will want to know how you will structure lesson activities to meet the students' learning needs. Briefly, provide a few examples of best-practice instruction you would use, e.g. learning stations, or jigsaw approach (see Table 26.1). Explain how you would incorporate accommodations for ELL and special education students. Lastly, describe how you will reflect on the effectiveness of the lesson and what steps you will take to improve it.

Why should you be hired over other job applicants?

This question is commonly asked in interviews, along with its variants: what makes you unique? What special skills, talents, or experiences do you have that can benefit the students and/or school? Before going into any interview, you should give these questions serious consideration. Start by reviewing whether you applied any of the strategies identified in this book:

- Increasing your endorsements and certifications (see Strategies 8 and 9)

- Continuing professional development (see Strategy 21)

- Enhancing your work experience through substitute teaching, coaching, or tutoring (see Strategy 11)

- Taking reasonable risks inside and/or outside the classroom (see Strategies 23-27)

- Volunteering in the community (see Strategy 31)

- Building an educational touchstone (see Strategy 34)

- Pursing professional and personal interests (see Strategies 8 and 12)

Yet other ways can distinguish you from your peers. For instance, your personal and professional work experiences outside academia may set you apart. Traveling and living aboard are other valuable experiences that may distinguish you as a unique job applicant.

A Principal's Perspective

Certainly, we all desire to hit a homerun during our interview. However, some job candidates are not prepared for an interview. Principal Kathryn Hutchinson shares some amusing real-life examples of bad interview techniques that you should avoid.

1) During the interview, you hit on one of the interviewers and ask for their phone number.

2) You express your concern about actually getting the job because it will interfere with the kitchen remodel you just started.

3) You disclose that you really wanted a teaching job at another school, but that school did not have a coaching position. Therefore, you will do this job until the coaching position opens up at the other school.

4) You are on so much medication you believe you were once a covert military operative, and, presumably, it's why the position doesn't appear anywhere on your application or resume.

5) You're showing so much cleavage that Oprah wants you on her next makeover show.

6) You describe in detail how you are not over your divorce because she left you for another man. This has caused big trust issues, and this has become a big hostile battle between you and your wife.

7) Your writing sample has no capital letters and very few
    punctuation marks.

On a more serious note, Principal Hutchinson continues with some good interviewing techniques.

Be on time to your interview, and allow extra time for traffic. But, it's not the end of the world if you're late, interviewers will understand if there are extenuating circumstances, such as power outages and illness (getting lost is a less extenuating circumstance).

It is not always essential to ask a question at the end of an interview. If you do, ask ONE good question that shows your insight into the school. I recall one occasion where the job candidate asked almost as many questions at the end of the interview as was asked during it. She didn't get the job. There's plenty of time to ask everything you like after you've been made an offer and are deciding to take the job.

Lastly, remember the interviewer WANTS YOU TO BE THE ONE. The interviewers probably don't enjoy the process of hiring and the quicker they can fill the position the happier they will be. At the interview, they are actually looking for reasons to hire you, so relax and find a way to be yourself. But, don't take it personally if you're not chosen because truly, more often than not, it's not about you. A school with high-energy kids may find someone with a commanding presence a better fit over someone with the same qualifications, but with a barely audible voice and that fidgets. Keep the faith!

Kathryn Hutchinson, High School Principal

Recommended Book

Teacher Interviews: How to Get Them and How to Get Hired!
By Robert W. Pollock, Ed.D.
Advanta Press, Martinsville, New Jersey, 2001.

Practice with Videotaping and Virtual Interviews

A fabulous, insightful technique to prepare you for an interview is to videotape yourself in a mock interview. With a family member or a friend, find a quiet spot to set up a video camera to record your answers to some of the interview questions given above. While this may seem awkward at first, by reviewing the videotape you will see yourself from the point of view of the interviewer. In reviewing your performance, analyze your mannerisms and voice inflections. For instance, are you saying "um" a lot? Are you slouching in your chair? Are you not speaking loudly enough for the interviewer to hear you? Do you show confidence and passion in your responses? Does your desire to teach children show through? Do you seem confident that you are the "right one" for this job? Ask your family member or friend to provide feedback on your performance. They may find something to improve on that you have overlooked.

The 'virtual' interview is a nontraditional approach to interview practice. There are a number of websites that provide virtual interviews, for example, Monster.com. These websites present you frequently asked interview questions. While this is helpful in practicing for unanticipated questions, the questions are not specifically geared towards education.

Prepare for Phone Interviews

Many of my colleagues interviewed over the telephone. Here are some suggestions and hints in case you have a scheduled phone interview:

- Smile during your interview. Years in the customer service business have taught me that it makes a significant difference in your tone, inflection, and speech on the phone. The interviewers will hear your smile!

- Arrange a quiet area, away from distractions, for your interview. Notify everyone not to disturb you during your phone interview and lock away any noisy pets.

- Dress professionally. It may be easier to be in sweats, but professional dress will help to put you in the right frame of mind, and you may sound more professional as well.

- Take notes during the interview—this will help you to better focus and listen.

- Have your resume and portfolio readily available.

- Practice beforehand as if you were preparing for a face-to-face interview.

Strategy 46

Leverage Your Research

The way to do research is to attack the facts
at the point of greatest astonishment.

— Celia Green

Research, research, research. Make a determined effort to learn all you can about the local community and your target school. In doing your research and data mining, identify ways in which you could contribute value to the school. In other words, what can you bring to the table? How can you help close certain academic gaps? How can you fulfill specific school or student needs? For instance, you note a significant upward trend in Filipino student enrollment. Imagine you have lived in the Philippines and you know the language, or you have run an after-school Asian student association club. By pairing your research with your distinctive experiences you will be able to further differentiate yourself in the interview. By discussing these points, you will demonstrate to the interviewer that you did your homework, you have analytical and problem-solving skills, and you are able to provide a service another job candidate may not.

As you sift through your research, digest the data you have collected. One way to do this is with a sheet of paper. Draw a line down the middle, on the left hand side list 5-10 striking statistics from your research, e.g., the dropout rate is increasing by 10% each year. On the right hand side, jot down possible ways that you could address those statistics. For example, assume you have noted the above dropout rate on the left hand side of the paper. On the right hand side of your paper, you may write down your experience in managing a distance learning, credit retrieval program at your previous school and you believe this could significantly reduce the dropout rate. Bring these notes to your interview to remind yourself how you bring value to the students and school. When you are asked in the interview, "Why should I hire you?" you now have the necessary response that directly targets school-related metrics.

Develop Community Awareness

Thoroughly investigate the community in which your target school is located. Many beginning teachers desire to relocate and teach outside their hometown. Other beginning teachers have to expand their job search beyond their hometown to land their dream job. No matter what the circumstances are, the out-of-town preservice teacher is at a disadvantage over the hometown job applicant. Some basic research can minimize this disadvantage.

Read the local newspapers, especially the education section, to familiarize yourself with the community. Many newspapers, and their archives, are now available on-line.

Find out about the school's neighborhood, read up on such things as demographics, cost of living, and quality of life. In a large city, neighborhoods can differ greatly from each other. The simplest way to uncover this specific information is to visit Yahoo's® Real Estate website (www.realestate.yahoo.com/neighborhoods) where you can research any community by city name or zip code.

While the Internet can give you a quantitative look at the local community, it falls short of providing any sense of local culture. If you can, visit the school and some of the surrounding neighborhoods. Stop by a local café or restaurant and observe the patrons; take notice of their ethnicity, their socio-economic background, and how they interact with each other. This will help you understand the students' home culture.

Research Your Target School

Finding out about the local community is important, but researching the school district and your target school is vital. There are no excuses for not being prepared for a scheduled interview. What was once a laborious process of fact-finding has been revolutionized and simplified by the Internet. Most of the information that you will need can be easily found at SchoolMatters (www.schoolmatters.com), a website service by Standard & Poor's®. SchoolMatters provides the following information: school overview, student performance, college preparation, No Child Left Behind performance, and the school environment.

In viewing research websites, such as SchoolMatters, familiarize yourself with basic information, such as grade levels and the number of students served by the school. Remember to try to connect this data to your experiences, skills, and special abilities. For example, do you have experience working in a school of this size?

Compare the school's standardized test scores, broken out by subject, of to other schools, the district, and state test scores. Analyze the testing trends over the last few years. This can help you determine how well the students are doing, how well they are learning, and if they are improving over time. Review this information with these questions in mind:

- What subject scores (math, science, reading, writing, etc.) is the school strong in compared to the district and state?

- What subject scores is the school weak in compared to the district and state?

- How would you describe the overall student performance compared to the district and state?

- What data trends in the student performance strike you as interesting?

- What experiences do you have that address the school's student performance?

- What skills and abilities do you have that address some the concerns in student performance?

Examine the data on how well the school prepares the students for college. Look at how many students take Advanced Placement (AP) classes and how well the students faired on the SAT and ACT tests. Any experience you have in teaching an AP class could differentiate you from other job candidates. Or perhaps you note that very few students take the ACT and SAT, you could mention that you have an interest in increasing awareness of the ACT and SAT by placing informational posters in the hallways and classrooms, and sending home parent letters. In addition, you could offer to hold several ACT and SAT preparation classes in an effort to boost participation. These are just two examples of creative solutions you can offer to improve student performance.

Next, determine if your target school has met the Average Yearly Progress (AYP) as required under the No Child Left Behind Act (see Strategy 11). If the school is not meeting requirements, at what stage is the school in their compliance? Has the school completed a plan for school improvement?

Further, use the research websites to identify student enrollment trends, teacher profiles, class sizes, and staffing trends in the school. Here are some guiding questions:

- What is the make-up of the student population?

- What are the trends in enrollment?

- How would you describe the staffing? Is the staff older with a lot of experience? Alternatively, is the staff younger with less experience?

- What percentage of the staff holds Master's Degrees?

You should also visit the school's website to familiarize yourself with the school's mission statement and any school-wide initiatives. While many schools do not see their mission statement as the driver of change, a few schools do take their mission statements very seriously. In an interview, you may be asked a question relating to the mission statement. Now is the time to think about how you would use the school's mission statement to drive your teaching and classroom management. Many schools also include information on their websites about school-wide initiatives, such as the implementation of a new reading program or a movement towards integration. Whatever the school's initiative may be, see if you can relate your background, education, and work experience to it. Lastly, browse the other information on the website. You may find gems like archived school newsletters that can provide valuable insight into the school's culture, strengths, and areas in need of improvement.

"Why should I hire you?" "What makes you unique as a job candidate?" "How will you add value to the students and school?" By immersing yourself in the school's data, metrics, and initiatives, you will have a better understanding of how your experiences and skills will directly benefit the students and school.

Then, instead of floundering while trying to answer these common interview questions, you will now be able to provide a well-researched, data-driven, and targeted response that will certainly impress the interviewers.

Strategy 47

- - - - - - - - - -

Go For a Trial Run

**When I have fully decided that a result is worth getting
I go ahead of it and make trial after trial until it comes.**

— Thomas A. Edison

Teachers prepare their students before a test with reviews, fun activities, alternative assessments, and quizzes. Coaches condition their teams through countless drills and practices before the big game. Why bother with all this practice and preparation? Because practice builds awareness, confidence, and skills, and it reduces the likelihood of failure. Why not then apply the same principle – practice – to the interview process?

I learned this strategy from an executive that currently works at a large oil company. When this man graduated college with an engineering degree he discovered he was horrible at interviewing. He told me that he would get sweaty, and choked up. As a result, he was not getting any of the jobs he interviewed for, despite his excellent qualifications. He realized he needed practice, but without the high pressure of applying for a job he really wanted. So, he applied for a job in an industry that was not of much interest to him. When he went to the interview, he felt more comfortable knowing that his sole purpose was to get practice at interviewing, but not to actually get the job. During his interview, he performed well. Finally, the interviewer asked him why this job was of interest to him. He honestly replied that he was trying to get better at interviewing and that was why he had applied. The interviewer was so impressed with his interview responses, his honesty, and, most importantly, his desire to improve, that he was hired the next day.

I adopted this strategy when I had completed my teacher education program and was looking for a job. My passion was to teach business, but I kept my options open for other teaching positions in topics for which I had endorsements. However, I also wanted interviewing experience, so I interviewed for social studies and history teaching positions in various high schools. I was not offered any of these jobs, but I did gain valuable insight and experience into the job seeking and interview process. When I applied for a job that I really wanted, I walked into the interview with increased confidence and determination and got the job.

When using this strategy, understand that there is a professional fine-line that you need to be careful not to cross. I encourage you to apply for jobs that you are qualified for, but may not be the exact job or location you were wishing for. You never know they may offer you the job. However, applying for any position for which you are not qualified will surely be unproductive for yourself and all parties involved.

Strategy 48

Dress Professionally

Is my dress too short?

— Victoria Beckham

If you really want the job, you should dress appropriately for the interview. Your dress is a reflection of your professionalism and a demonstration of how much you care about the job you are interviewing for. It astounds me that even today I hear stories of preservice teachers interviewing in shorts or jeans. And this is not an issue just with preservice teachers. One principal told me of a teacher with over ten years experience that arrived at an interview wearing a t-shirt and a baseball cap, unshaven and with a plumber's crack. The principal quietly passed on that unprofessional teacher. This will always be true for unprofessionally dressed job candidates, no matter how well qualified they are.

Many preservice teachers wonder just what professional interviewing attire consists of. Tables 48.1 and 48.2 have some specific guidelines to help you put together your professional interviewing outfit.

Table 48.1

Men's Interview Attire	
Recommended:	*Acceptable:*
Business suit, dress shirt, tie, belt, and dress socks	Sweater, slacks, dress shirt, belt, tie, and dress socks
Sport coat, dress slacks with dress shirt, belt, tie, and dress socks	

Table 48.2

Women's Interview Attire	
Recommended:	*Acceptable:*
Business suit (slacks), blouse, and nylons, tights, or trouser socks	Slacks with blouse, sweater, and nylons, tights, or trouser socks
Business suit (skirt), blouse, and nylons, or tights	Slacks with blouse, jacket, and nylons, tights, or trouser socks
Business dress with sleeves, and nylons, or tights	Slacks with business blouse, and nylons, tights, or trouser socks
Business dress with blazer, or sweater, and nylons, or tights	Skirt with blouse, sweater, and nylons, or tights
	Skirt with blouse, jacket, and nylons, or tights
	Skirt with business blouse, and nylons, or tights

As you put your outfit together, be sure that everything coordinates. For instance, if your dress shoes are black then wear a black belt and avoid wearing white socks with your professional attire. For women, here are some further notes on clothing that should be avoided:

- Skirts more than 2" above the knee
- Shirts showing midriffs or cleavage, or see-through clothing
- Dresses with spaghetti straps without a jacket

Accessories, Piercings, and Tattoos

Many preservice teachers ask what is appropriate for accessories, piercings, and tattoos. Accessories such as jewellery are fine as long as they coordinate with your business outfit, and they are not flashy or too large. As for piercings, if it is possible you should remove any visible body piercings other than those in your ears, which you should limit to one or two. For the interview, make an effort to cover any visible tattoos.

Strategy 49

Hit a Homerun!

Do not hire a man who does your work for money, but him who does it for love of it.

— Henry David Thoreau

As I sat in the District office's waiting room, I remember thinking to myself this is it—the opportunity I have been waiting for. The job description was exactly what I had been looking for. I was highly qualified for this position and I knew I had a good chance of being hired. On the other hand, I realized this was my last shot at finding a decent teaching job. I had been looking for a teaching job for several months and it was now late August. School would be starting in less than a week. I certainly did not want to return to substitute teaching for another semester. I had to prove myself in this interview and show that I was capable of doing the job. Moreover, I had to demonstrate my intense passion for teaching children.

I was called into the interview room where the principal, department head, human resource personnel, and district official sat around the table. Admittedly, I was a little nervous, but not as much as I would have been if I hadn't had some practice interviews. After introductions, they began to spring questions at me. To this day, I do not remember what they asked me. But, I remember being in the state of mind that Michael Jordan called "being in the zone." In other words, I was on top of my game. I recall speaking from the heart, conversing passionately about teaching and demonstrating how my qualities and experiences set me apart from other teachers.

As I was returning home after the interview, I felt that if I was not hired for this job then I was not going to get any job. But, I was confident that I was going to be hired. Two days later, I received the call from the principal offering me the position. If you were to ask me what made the difference among this interview and job and the rest of the interviews and jobs I didn't get, I would say it boiled down to having and showing passion.

Do you have passion?

There is no doubt that teaching is a tough job. It entails hard work, long hours, and countless commitments, accompanied by unjust compensation. Not to mention those teaching days when you feel like giving up. The distinguishing factor between the teachers that continue and those that quit is passion: passion for the children, passion for making a difference in a child's life, and passion for teaching.

It is this passion that principals want to see in prospective teachers. As a prospective teacher, you need to let your passion come across in the interview. Your enthusiasm should be obvious in your responses to the interview questions.

You can also show your passion by retelling a story about a particular student's success and explaining how such successes motivate you to teach.

Be passionate as you explain why you think you would be great at teaching in that particular subject or area. For example, you may be passionate about special education because a close relative had autism and you understand the importance of providing a safe and caring learning environment for exceptional children. Whatever your passion may be, be sure that you do not leave the interview without somehow demonstrating to the interviewers your commitment and enthusiasm for the children and teaching. You only have one shot at this interview, so make it a homerun!

A Principal's Perspective

You can see it in their eyes, you can hear it in their words, in their stories, and it casts an aura around them. It is one of the things I look and listen for when I interview a candidate to work with my elementary students.

In today's market, there are handfuls of excellent candidates for an elementary position. With the multitude of educational colleges that train teachers, I often wonder do they see it in their students. Are they able to see a fire for teaching, something that cannot be taught, but centers itself in the very core of their work? That core is passion!

We are in a time of restructuring, aligning curriculum, differentiating instruction, assessing learning and helping young students become life-long learners. The challenges presented daily are overwhelming, demanding, and endless. Our students come with all types of backgrounds, from the affluent to the impoverished, from single parents, divorced parents, grandparents, to no parents. Connecting with each child and building a trusting relationship to enable the learning process is a challenge that changes with each student.

A teacher's passion supports them through these hard times. It is this inner core of strength that propels them to meet each day with purpose, belief, and dedication. It is this inner core that will help them see thorough the multitude of demands of accountability to what they want most for each child.

Passion is the key to resilience, it is the antidote for burnout, it is the fire that makes this job the best in the world.

Cris Welch, Elementary School Principal

Strategy 50

- - - - - - - - - - - - -

Control the Interview Process

Those who are blessed with the most talent
don't necessarily outperform everyone else.
It's the people with follow-through who excel.

— Mary Kay Ash

Picture this scenario. You are sitting in the main office of the school awaiting an interview for a teaching job you desperately want. While you feel nervous, you also feel self-assured in your ability to excel in this teaching position. You reflect on the valuable, diverse experience and skills you have developed since starting your preservice study program. You are proud of the social network you have developed, and which, in fact, landed you this interview. Furthermore, you are pleased with your ability to organize coursework, contacts, teaching portfolios, certification paperwork, and teaching application requirements. You believe all your effort has finally paid off.

Then the moment comes and your name is called for the interview. Immediately your heart begins pounding, your palms become clammy and you try to hide this unpleasant reality by discreetly wiping them on your pants. You enter into a room with five individuals seated around a large conference table. You smile and begin systematically shaking their hands. Upon finishing the pleasantries and sitting down, the interview begins. The interviewers introduce themselves, explain the interview process, and then start asking questions.

One after another the questions come. Because you have practiced, you respond in a thoughtful, confident, and insightful manner. Eventually, the interview ends; again, you smile, shake their hands, and thank them for the wonderful opportunity. Before you know it, you are sitting in your car wondering what just happened, and questioning if it went okay. In retrospect, the whole experience seems a blur.

A few days have past since your interview, and finally, the phone rings. The principal is calling to tell you the interview team has decided to go with someone else. The principal thanks you for your time and hangs up. You are dumbfounded. Self-doubt begins to creep in and you ask yourself these questions:

"Why didn't I get the job?"

"Did I say something wrong during the interview?"

"What could I have done differently?"

"Am I really cut out for this?"

This scenario, although very real, is problematic in numerous ways. Namely, the interviewee was not in control at any point of the interview process, but simply went through it, and then left without asking why he/she did not get the job.

This state of wondering and self-doubt is not productive. The key lesson in applying for teaching positions is to understand that losing is sometimes inevitable, but the trick is not to make a habit of it. There are some simple strategies to remaining in control and wrapping-up the interview in your favor.

Slow Down

The first step in taking back control, and not "just passing through" the interview process, is to slow down. Pay attention to your breathing, take deep, controlled breaths before going into the room where the interview will take place. Breathe in through your nose and out through your mouth. This technique will relax you, steady your heart rate, and put you in a better state of mind for your interview.

Bring your research notes with your skill sets and how they match with the needs of the school and review them just before you go in to the interview (see Strategy 46). This will serve as a quick reminder of some points that you should address.

When you go into the interview, and after you greet everyone, ask if you can take some notes during the interview. Quickly jot down the names and positions of the interviewers. This will be critical information for writing thank-you notes after the interview. During the interview, write down any important points made.

Likewise, make notes when something you said may have caused confusion or was construed differently than your original intent. You can clarify these points later in your thank-you notes. By applying these simple acts, you become a more active participant in the process and less of a bystander.

Make the Ask

A relatively simple, but highly effective way to close an interview is to ask for the teaching job. In the business world, the most significant factor that contributes to substandard performance in sales is not closing the sale, or in other words, not asking for the sale. The same principle applies to interviewing. In essence, you are selling yourself, your skills, and experience. Towards the end of the interview, briefly restate your desire to teach in the target school and outline the 2-3 reasons why you are a qualified candidate. Finally, thank the interviewers for their time.

Follow-up Immediately

Once your interview is complete, differentiate yourself further by sending out thank-you notes to all the interviewers on that same day. Bring a stack of thank-you notes and several postage stamps with you to your interview. Then, find a place where you feel comfortable to write the thank-you notes, whether that place is your car or a nearby coffee shop. Refer back to the notes you took during the interview and make every effort to personalize each thank-you note. Mention something that will help your interviewer remember you among all the other interviewers. Here are a few suggestions:

1) Address an issue that arose during your interview, especially when the topic favors your qualifications. For instance, your ELL endorsement was discussed as an asset due to the rising number of ELL students in the school.

2) Overcome objections by responding to an interviewer's major concern in detail that was not possible during the interview.

3) Highlight your skills or experiences that qualify you as a strong candidate and will differentiate you from other candidates.

Now relax, all you have to do is drop off the thank-you notes in the mail and wait for the all-important phone call.

Handling the Phone Call

The final step in the interview process is notification of whether you have received the job, or whether you are scheduled for a second interview. The notification usually comes in the form of a phone call, but sometimes it may be a letter. Before you receive that phone call, there are steps you should take to prepare yourself.

Let us first examine the worst scenario. Assume the principal phones you to inform you that you will not be filling the teaching position. While this is a crushing blow, take control of the conversation and learn from it. First, be extremely professional and courteous—you never know when another position may materialize at the same school. Thank the principal for their time, and ask what specifically you could improve on in the interview or on your resume for next time. Many times the principal will be frank and give you fantastic, constructive advice. Remember to listen, and, most importantly, be receptive to what the principal is saying. It is not to your advantage to be defensive. As in the teaching process, you can take this advice, revise your approach a little, and confidently prepare for your next interview.

In the optimistic scenario, let us assume that you land your dream teaching job. Typically, the principal phones you, requesting your references. Take this request as an extremely positive sign. Understand, though, that many principals cannot offer you the job until your reference check is complete. Therefore, it is important to have your references, with primary and alternate contact numbers, with you at all times because you simply do not know when the principal will call. Finally, thank the principal for giving you this opportunity and then, after the phone call, go celebrate—you have earned it!

References Cited

Cohen, L.M., & Gelbrich, J. (1999). Sample educational philosophy statements. Retrieved August 11, 2006, Web site: http://oregonstate.edu/instruct/ed416/sample.html

Collins, J.C. (2001). *Good to great: Why some companies make the leap, and others don't.* New York, NY: HarperBusiness.

Conley, D.T. (2005). *College knowledge: What it really takes for students to succeed and what we can do to get them ready.* San Francisco, CA: Jossey-Bass.

Curwin, R.L., & Mender, A.N. (1993). Discipline with dignity. *Alexandria, VA: Association for Supervision and Curriculum Development.*

Darling, D. (2003). *The networking survival guide: get the success you want by tapping into the people you know.* New York: McGraw-Hill.

Federal Student Aid. (2006). Teacher loan forgiveness program: FFEL and direct loan programs. Retrieved July 13, 2007, from Federal Student Aid Web site: http://studentaid.ed.gov/PORTALSWebApp/students/english/cancelstaff.jsp

Gladwell, M. (2000). *The Tipping Point: How little things can make a big difference.* Boston, MA: Little, Brown and Company.

Gruber, K.J., Wiley, S.D., Broughman, S.P., Strizek, G.A., & Burian-Fitzgerald, M. (2002). School and staffing survey, 1999-2000: Overview of the data public, private, public charter, and bureau of Indian affairs elementary and secondary schools. *National Center for Education Statistics.*

Hirsch, E. (2001). Teacher recruitment: Staffing classrooms with quality teachers. *State Higher Education Executive Officers.*

Krumme, G. (2005). Major categories in the taxonomy of educational objectives. Retrieved August 6, 2007, Web site: http://faculty.washington.edu/krumme/guides/bloom1.html

Pollock, R. (2001). *Teacher interviews: How to get them and to get hired!.* Martinsville, NJ: Advanta Press.

Thompson, J. (2002). *First-year teacher's survival kit: Ready-to-use strategies, tools & activities for meeting the challenges of each school day.* San Francisco, CA: Jossey-Bass.

Notes

1489781

Made in the USA